Dear Mary Jane,

Thank you for your love and faithfulness these fifteen years together. May God's love and guidance bless us in all future years as we raise our "little ones" and grow mature in our love.

Yours always, Love,

Ron.

Married Love in the Middle Years

Married Love
in the
Middle Years

James A. Peterson

Association Press / New York

MARRIED LOVE IN THE MIDDLE YEARS

First Printing — June 1968
Second Printing — November 1968

Publisher's stock number: 1673
Library of Congress catalog card number: 68-17773

Printed in the United States of America

To Audrey
who fills every hour of the second half of life
with the freshness of
childhood wonder and beauty
and with the wisdom of creative maturity

Preface

This book is the product of two strands of my experience; one comes from twenty years of counseling with middle-aged persons who have despaired of joy in their mid-years, and the other is in the research laboratory of gerontology, where problems of aging are subjected to the careful analysis of survey and statistical study. Both have contributed to the insights shared in these pages. Equally important are all the psychiatrists, geriatric specialists, psychologists, sociologists, educators, and others who have pondered creatively the problems of this period. It is possible to cite only a few of them in the text and in footnotes, but no author in this field is without debt to a great many persons.

This is not a scientific treatise about any one middle-range problem of aging. It is a general book to bring some of the findings and insights from science and the therapy desk to middle-aged individuals. The purpose of this book is to create an awareness in depth of the many aspects of adjustment problems during middle age. It does not attempt to bring anything new to, or advance theory in, the field. I am engaged in research on several specific problems of aging, but I have tried not to let either the vocabulary or the approach interfere with this effort to gather some helpful insights together to meliorate some of the problems of the middle-aged. The two types of effort are worthwhile, but they are entirely different.

I am indebted to Dr. James Birren for reading part of the manuscript, to Wilbur T. Blume and Frank Riley for helpful suggestions about style and content. I feel deeply my obligation to Miss Ima Pointer, who typed and retyped these chapters with acute attention to structure and form. And finally I wish to praise my wife, who gave up many weekends and part of her vacation so that this book could be completed.

James A. Peterson

Contents

CONTENTS

1

Middle-Age
Crisis

From one point of view, people in their middle years are in the prime of life. They are at the zenith of their productive capacities. The skill of their hands and the discipline of their minds have been honed by twenty years of adult living. Their paychecks have larger figures than ever before, and they are near the highest point in their occupational status. Socially and politically, their years of effort are rewarded, for they sit on the school board, the city council, and the church vestry. Their voices carry authority, and their social position is established. If their marriages have lasted this long, the chance for failure is very small. In the language of their teen-agers, "They have it made."

But when we look at people in their middle years from other perspectives, we see that they may not have it "made" at all. Their children are entering the last years of high school, military service, or college. While the parents still have major financial responsibility for their offspring, the chore of daily supervision in child rearing is over. The loving years of young parenthood have frequently dissolved in alienation and in overt or covert battles with the young. The psychic rewards of mothering or fathering children have been succeeded by the perplexities and strains of coping with the "hip" generation and its new morality and irreverence.

There is often another, more personal realization. Middle age is the time in life when men and women begin to be aware of the loss of physical zest, when the sexual drive is no longer so urgent, and when the urge to recapture youth makes the "playboy" philosophy attractive. They may be at their prime, but immediately beyond is the prospect of chronic illness, disability, and retirement. They lose more and more friends to "incidents" of heart failure, hypertension, and cancer. The battle to immobilize aging takes precedence over social or intellectual creativity, so that the promise of the prime of life is destroyed by anxiety over the loss of youth.

"MIDDLE AGE" IS YOUNGER THAN IT USED TO BE

These are some of the characteristics of middle age, but is it possible to identify this period in terms of age? Twenty-five years ago it was assumed that one was middle-aged between the ages of fifty and sixty-five because everyone who retired did so between sixty-five and seventy, and retirement ushered in yet another era. Incidence of physical disability and death rose so dramatically in the fifties that this seemed to be a natural beginning of "middle age"; however, several factors now seem to suggest a downward shift in dating middle age.

Changing Patterns of Work

Genesis tells us that man, because of his sin, was cast from the Garden of Eden and commanded henceforth to earn his bread by the sweat of his brow. And, indeed, throughout all history and even today in three quarters of the world, man labors from dawn until darkness for a precarious existence. But in the United States, technological advances have contracted work periods. The United Auto Workers in a recent contract negotiation succeeded in winning a new stipulation that under certain conditions, men may retire at fifty-five. Likewise, civil service workers on the Federal payroll may now retire at fifty-five. Some teachers, doctors, and other professionals have anticipated this trend, and a growing number of individuals have decided on a retirement career for the last quarter of their lives. An ever-lengthening period of education is now required to equip the next generation to work in a more and more complex system. The possibility of retiring at fifty-five, now a reality for a substantial number of our citizens, makes it possible for them to spend more of their years studying or at leisure than in paid employment! Middle age, then, would appear to be the years after one's career is established and immediately preceding retirement.

Changing Family Patterns

A second significant consideration is that the family life cycle has changed. The average couple complete child bearing by the age of twenty-six, and are in their early forties when the last child is adolescent. Fifty years ago children still dominated the family scene when their parents were in their fifties or even in their early sixties. Today younger members of the family leave home much earlier for military service, college, work, or marriage. But even more significant is the very real alienation of adolescents from their parents. When the young shift their loyalty from their parents to their friends, a new period in family life has begun.

Physiological Considerations

A third, physiological, consideration is the fact that many women enter the premenopausal period in their forties. Some men also reach a plateau in both physical energy and motivation at about the same time. Some authors suggest that the loss of vitality, imagination, and innovation begins around thirty-five. However, in view of the factors we have used to describe this period, thirty-five seems a little early to be called "middle-aged." Let us set the lower limit at forty, recognizing that the onset of the crisis described in this chapter may occur over a spread of five to ten years for different people.

THE PROBLEMS, AS SEEN IN A TYPICAL COUPLE

To be even more specific let me share with you a summary of a case at my clinic. Like all case material in this book, the names, the professions, and the locale have been radically altered; there is no possibility that the persons in this case could ever be identified. This is the ethical rule under which all therapists operate. But the psychological and social facts of the case are accurate, and it is these facts that have meaning in helping us pinpoint the problems of the middle years. Furthermore, every therapist is quick to point out that the general dimensions of such cases are very similar, even if the specific instances are unique. That means that this case could describe three dozen others we see every year, and is relevant in at least some of its details to almost every middle-aged couple.

Bill and Helen came in to talk about their two boys. Bill was forty-seven years of age; his wife, Helen, was forty-five. The two boys, Mike and Jim, were twenty-one and eighteen.

Bill was a division manager in an insurance company, where he had worked since he was twenty-one years of age. His hairline had receded halfway on one side, and the shiny spot was poorly covered because the rest of his hair was thinning and gray. While he was dressed neatly and had a trim figure, there was a bulge in front that indicated some good living or at least some loss of discipline at the table. He rarely smiled, but when he did, extensive gold repairs were very evident. His wife looked somewhat younger, but a few worry lines were etched on her face beneath her careful makeup.

After obtaining a general picture of their difficulties, I asked if I might speak with each of them alone in order to get a fair picture of how they both viewed the problem. Bill seemed apprehensive about what his wife would say, and she seemed to be bursting with things she wanted to say.

Helen welcomed the opportunity to talk privately. She admitted that their boys had problems: their grades were inferior and their companions not exactly the ones she and her husband would choose. On the whole, it seemed to me, the boys were not much different than many others. The real problem was Bill. She suspected that there was something else causing him such hostility, and she made her own diagnosis. It was her firm belief that he had what her friends called "the middle-age itch." She suspected that he was having an affair and that his anger was really guilt which he could not tolerate. She did not seem unduly upset at the thought of his having an affair, but she was unhappy about his taking it out on the boys. When I asked her very specifically about proof that her husband was having an affair, she answered by saying that most men of his age did so.

She confided that their own sexual life had dwindled away and that it had been increasingly frustrating to her during the last years because of her husband's growing impotency. She cried when I questioned her about her general satisfaction with the marriage. She felt that there was little left for her in life. When the boys had begun to fashion their own lives, she had turned to her husband with plans for a renewed life between them, but his absorption in his business and his sexual failure left her with an empty feeling. She said she was trying not to turn to her boys for emotional support because they now had to live their own lives. She expressed her hope for help, not for the boys alone, but also for her husband and herself.

When I saw Bill, he was most curious about what I had discussed with his wife. I explained to him our rules regarding such conferences and then asked why he was so anxious. He was somewhat chagrined at that question, and grew very defensive. I assured him that the only purpose of our meeting was to help his family, that I did not keep score on grievances, and that if he wanted to ease the strain with his boys and his wife, it would help if he could be candid with me. He avoided the issue and went into a long question about the structuring of our interviews. He wanted reassurance that I would see them together from then on. When I interpreted to him both his evasion of my invitation to candor and self-examination and his rather obvious defensiveness about his wife's having any further opportunities to tell me about their life from her point of view, he admitted he was worried. Then he was silent. I waited quite a while. I did not think he was sulking, but rather measuring his next step.

His decision was to evade any reference to himself. He asked what we might do to help his boys, as he felt he had lost all relationship with them. After some discussion we agreed that we would invite the boys to participate in the next conference and try to discover how communication could be restored and the relationship improved. Bill thought that this concluded our conference and stood up. I remained seated and looked inquiringly at him. He hesitated, and I asked him whether this were really all that was troubling him. He flushed, sat down, started to speak, and then stopped. We sat silent for some time. He was probably thinking about what his wife might have said regarding their sexual life, but he hesitated to bring it up if she had not said anything. He finally burst out: "I am having a hell of a time! . . . I . . ." That outburst helped him and he went on:

As a young fellow in the Air Force we flew training planes that could only go up five thousand feet . . . that was their limit. I feel about my life what I felt then . . . no matter what I do I've reached the limit of my life . . . all the young fellows coming into the company know more than I do . . . and I feel outmoded . . . like a misfit. I don't feel needed anymore, my wife . . . she needs me but I'm not any good with her . . . I'm so mixed up and depressed that generally I don't help her. I suppose she told you that our sexual life is nothing, but that's only part of it . . . I used to have energy . . . play tennis all day and dance all night. Now I get pains around my chest . . . I haven't told her that. You know I even thought it might help me to date my secretary awhile and win my confidence back . . . she's divorced and lonely . . . and young, but I don't . . . I might even fail with her . . . and then I'd know I really was over the hill.

This case is not unusual. It contains many of the problems middle-aged persons endure. Bill's various complaints are not unique. During middle age both men and women experience a rather dramatic decrease in energy levels. Their store of energy is exhausted sooner than it used to be, and it takes longer to restore it. While they may have played three hard sets of tennis and enjoyed the rugged race of singles competition in their thirties, they settle for two sets of doubles in the forties and fifties. There are also many sensory losses, with increasing difficulty in reading, hearing, and fine coordination. They note with annoyance that they have to hold a book at arm's length or within a few inches of the nose in order to distinguish the letters. They find themselves dozing off at lectures, concerts, or movies. Gray hairs are noted ruefully by the man and with panic by his wife. He grudgingly orders a suit with a larger waistband, and she secretly does exercises to modify the middle-age spread. All these add to the panic they experience on the wedding anniversary evening, when sex is no longer the thrill they both expect. Youth and sexual capacity are waning, and life seems to be "slipping away."

The Wife's Problems

Helen faced a common problem in her efforts to find substitute satisfactions for those she had received from her children. She failed to find them in renewed communion with her husband.

As we have noted, the average mother completes child bearing by age twenty-six. The last child is in school by the time she is thirty; he is in high school and certainly psychologically "away" by the time she is forty-five. Half of the families in our country have launched the last child from home by the time the mother is fifty. She has finished the entire cycle of child bearing, rearing, and launching at an age when Grandmother was still bearing children or caring for little ones. She has almost half of her married life still ahead of her, but barren of purpose. The children that dominated every hour of planning, absorbed her affection, gave her a sense of achievement and fulfillment are gone. Like Helen, she has nowhere to turn for emotional response but to her husband. If the couple are to make up for the gap left by their children's departure, they have to substitute new patterns of activity for those that previously involved the entire family as well as to renew emotional commitments often forgotten or directed towards the children.

Not all mothers have devoted so much time to their children. An increasing number have turned much of the child care over to nurseries, kindergartens, and "housemothers" and have escaped into the marketplace. This is not strictly accurate when speaking of mothers of very young children because only 17 per cent of them are gainfully employed. The low mark of female employment is reached at age twenty-nine, when the child-bearing period is completed. It does not reach its next high point until thirty-four, when the last child is in kindergarten. A high percentage of married women between the ages of thirty-four and sixty work. This significant fact is one that concerns the middle-aged group under discussion. Twenty years ago employment of married females rose until age forty and then began a steady decrease to age sixty. Today there is no decrease between forty and sixty at all. There is another group of married women who work outside the home, but for no pay. They are the ones who year by year staff hospitals, schools, churches, clinics, and clubs with volunteer help. They are away from home almost as much as those with regular working hours, but their schedules are probably more flexible. The problems of middle age are somewhat different for women who are gainfully employed or who devote their lives to charitable interests than for those who have stayed at home and focused on their children.

The problem of the wife who works, whether for pay or not, is that of conflict with her husband. The impact of female employment on marital satisfaction has been researched and debated strenuously for at least twenty-five years. Extreme statements are heard from proponents of two extremes. There are some feminists who feel that no woman achieves her full potential unless she has a paid job in which she may move without hindrance up the occupational and status ladder. There are others who denounce female employment on both economic and psychological grounds. They feel that working women "castrate" men, destroy their marriages, and penalize their children. Some sober evidence exists, which we shall cite later to clarify this issue.

The woman's problem in defining what her position ought to be is complicated by the physiological changes that inevitably occur. She may have to adjust to the shock of building a new way of life because of loss of meaningful intimate relationships with children just at the period when she is called upon to cope with strange physiological sensations. While a man may feel panic and question his value as a sexual partner when his virility fails him, the menopause is an inescapable statement to the woman that the function of child bearing, for which she was born, is forever over. With the atrophy of the ovaries comes an awareness that a major aspect of her basic creativity is gone. Coming as it does just after or even while her last child is leaving home, it reinforces the notion that her life work may be finished. Even if she has dreaded and avoided pregnancy for the preceding fifteen years, she still experiences shock at the loss of her "femininity."

With this deeper psychic disturbance there are also physical symptoms, such as profuse perspiration, hot flushes and flashes, deeply annoying nerve irritability, irregular menstrual periods, exhaustion and fatigue, which all combine to make her miserable. All of these may interfere with sexual activity and contribute to whatever tension already exists between her husband and herself. Both the marital and the physiological stress may result in feelings of unworthiness, loss of significant role, and, sometimes, feelings of persecution. Minute neurotic tendencies with which she has lived all her life now grow into full-blown fears or conflicts, and she may rage, sulk, or withdraw. Her friends may subtly avoid her, and her husband may cultivate the closeness of others. If the alienation process is severe and her hormonal imbalance profound, she may lapse into a profound depression for months or years. Even if she does not display radical neurotic or psychotic tendencies, and most women do not, her exaggerated sensitivity, weeping spells, and general lassitude may be most difficult for her husband either to understand or to tolerate.

What Bothers the Husband?

But Bill had his own problems to face at this time, as do most husbands in the mid-years. Life had been somewhat different for him. It is true that he had worked long and hard to give his children medical care, opportunities for development, and education. He had nursed his insurance policies against the children's needs in case something happened to him. He had exulted in their success and worried about their choice of dating and marriage partners. But over all, he had been involved in other satisfying experiences in the community and in his occupation.

By the time he pays the last bills for his sons' education, he will be at the peak of his vocational achievement. Now that he is middle-aged, he is earning more than he did when he was younger, and more than he will later. He is now absorbed in the final drive for status and occupational recognition, and he has his own problems in this arena. He may be rather completely caught up in his work and in the struggle to accumulate the things that appeal to vanity. He may already have seen the limit of his potential achievement and begun to resent his investment of an enormous amount of energy, hope, and devotion to a success he may never achieve. In a society in which status is conferred on executive position or professional distinction, the vast majority are automatically excluded from achieving the final accolade. Yet in the process of striving the man too often develops a tunnel vision, which focuses only on work and excludes much time with his wife and children or for the development of larger interests. If, by middle age, this persistent chase has excluded any real cultivation of intimacy with his mate, he finds little comfort or closeness at home. Instead, the accumulation of neglect has indeed resulted in the "disenchantment" described earlier, and there is only a habitualized superficiality between him and his wife, as well as a polite, but resentful response from his grown children, who are all too well aware of his real status. When he begins to assess the meaning of his investment of time and energy, it is too late, the children are gone, and his wife is often alienated.

When the male reaches a plateau in his occupational achievement, when he senses a partial loss of his most cherished male possession—his potency, when he observes his no-longer-youthful face and feels the decline in energy, when he senses part of his motivation departing with his children, his mounting anxiety may reach a point of panic. He reviews his life and sorrows over the unfulfilled dreams of early manhood and the boredom of marriage. He may determine to prove to himself that he is still a man. A great many middle-aged men move towards other women to find answers to needs for reassurance and affection.

There is another aspect to this problem for the middle-aged man and woman in our society today that will probably not occur again. They grew up at the beginning of the sexual revolution, and did not feel its impact until far into marriage. Both men and women in this age group evidence great ambivalence about sex. They have never had sufficient knowledge or acceptance to be completely sure of their sexual identity or free in expressing their libido. Their early initiation to sex was limited, covert, and obscure. Sex for them was linked by church and community with sin, and few have been able to cut the chain. In the meantime Hugh Hefner, editor of *Playboy*, and others have been proclaiming that the salvation of living is to be found in sex. As a result, many middle-aged men and women feel passed over by life and covet more satisfaction than they have achieved.

Psychiatrists like Edmund Bergler, who wrote about and studied American sexual mores, believe that almost every male tries to recapture his adolescent sexual zest in his forties or fifties in the belief that social and sexual contact with a woman younger than his aging wife will reawaken sexual potentials which are not dead but only dormant. Thus the panic felt by the middle-aged man at loss of hair, need for thicker glasses, loss of energy, and occasional impotency often propels him into an affair with a younger woman. This activity is not a sudden discovery of a soul mate who understands him, nor an indication of an inferior marital relationship, but rather a sexual search for the "fountain of youth." On deeper and less conscious levels, an affair at middle age may be described as a challenge to death. The man who equates life force with sexual potency must prove to himself that he is as virile and attractive as he was at twenty-two.

Still another aspect in the motivation of many middle-aged men who climb in and out of strange beds is that they have combined feelings of their own aging and of hostility toward their wives. Marriage is a long and complex process of role adjustment, of compromise on values, and perhaps of the growth of profound compassion for the other. In marriages where any of these processes are arrested and failing, a residue of frustration and bitterness exists. By middle age there may be accommodation to frustration, but more often it results in rancid intolerance. Sex becomes a weapon in the battle. Sexual withholding magnifies earlier blows to self-esteem. Thus an affair in middle age is often a weapon for the discharge of hostility. This accounts for the fact that both men and women who engage in adultery usually contrive to let their marital partners know of their unfaithfulness. But there is more than one explanation. In some cases an affair is a symbol of surrender, a statement about the sterility of efforts to improve the marriage, as though the adulterer were saying, "I give up with you. I've tried and it's no good; there may yet be some small happiness for me with someone else." This is often a forlorn expectation, and the results are often more bitter than sweet.

The Loss of Emotional Support

While listening closely to Bill and Helen, I said that they seemed to have lost their ability to talk with one another, that there was little warmth between them and certainly no emotional support for each other. I said that if a couple stayed married until this period of life there is little statistical chance for divorce, and that is an accurate statement. But this does not mean that staying together is very rewarding.

A long-term sociological study of marriage in the middle years summarizes the mood of the relationship as that of "disenchantment." In the careful study made by Robert O. Blood, Jr., and Donald M. Wolfe in Detroit in 1962 only 6 per cent of the wives were very satisfied with their marriages after twenty-two years of living with their husbands.[1] It is not just that satisfaction wanes; the couple literally become disengaged, with decrease in shared leisure time and general loss of mutual activities. They do not talk as much, discuss problems or experiences in the same detail, or love as much. Bergler stated that every man during middle age is engaged in extramarital affairs.[2] That claim seems exaggerated in the light of other statistical studies, but Kinsey's figure of fifty per cent who engage in adultery indicates that many men seek tender satisfaction away from their own bedrooms. All these facts are indicators that the low divorce rate—twenty per hundred marriages—is no real measure of the degree of frustration that exists. A more accurate summary might be that half of those who do not get a divorce settle for "dreary compromise."

The average middle-aged couple have just finished or are about to finish child launching. They have been occupied for twenty years in the care and nurture of children. This has occupied most of their waking hours, dominated their economic planning, and conditioned their leisure-time pursuits. At the conclusion of child launching comes a radical loss of purpose, economic demand, and life satisfaction as well as a daily need for redefinition of family goals, family structure, and family activity change. The husband and wife are alone back where they were at the beginning of their marriage, with no emotional resources other than each other. It is a jarring disruption of life pattern—so jarring, in fact, that many men and women cannot let go of their children. This causes all kinds of problems to the psychological growth of their youth and, later, to the success of their offsprings' marriage.

Relationships With Grown Children

There is, of course, no reason why contact cannot exist between a couple and their grown, married children. The problem of helping children establish autonomy while still enjoying their fellowship in a reversal of roles is not an easy one, but many parents accomplish just that. If the married son or daughter has not moved too far away in the pursuit of his or her own economic welfare, happy times can be had on weekends, holidays, and birthdays. There is still a loose-knit helping network between parents and married children. Financial help by parents is far more common than advice, and this is a reversal since Grandfather's time. If the son or daughter has not developed too much hostility in adolescence, the cultivation of close-ness between the two generations can be rewarding indeed. The rapport is a good one when the older generation is referred to as "Grandmother and Grandfather" and not "the in-laws." To fully understand the child's treatment of his parents, it is essential to look carefully into the relationships he had in the family before he left. If, for instance, the child was the scapegoat of the family and the recipient of the projections of all other members, it is not surprising that he neglects them as soon as he can. If another child in another family resents his parents' quarreling to the extent that he makes an early and poor marriage, it is not likely that the two families will have substantial contacts when he is gone. Or if there has been a family struggle for power, in which the children lined up with the mother in her neurotic battle with the father, it is not likely that he will go out of his way to encourage further contacts once they have left the fray. In still other cases the two sets of in-laws are so jealous of their rights with the newly married pair that they count the times the young couple spend with the other in-laws and insist on equal treatment. Such posture is not destined to make for happy inter-family unity or enjoyment. These are all illustrations of the fact that family life is a cumulative movement in time and that the sorrows or joys of middle age are partially the harvest of earlier neurotic or wholesome interactions. In many cases there must be therapeutic intervention or the parents will sorrow all their lives and their children will carry a burden of guilt to the funerals of their father and mother.

Anxieties About Health

Both Bill and Helen were more concerned with their health than they admitted during that first interview. In this they also represent a large segment of their age group.

The more superficial signs of aging have real counterparts in health states. The incidence of disabling disease is lowest in the life cycle during the third decade. How shocking it is, then, when this group enters their forties, and their friends begin to die. The death rate continues to climb rapidly from this point on. The incidence of disabling disease is 54 per 1,000 between ages forty-five and fifty-four; it almost doubles to 93.8 from fifty-five to sixty-four. While the death rate climbs to 753 per 100,000 from forty-five to fifty-four, it almost triples in the next decade, when it is 1,737 per 100,000. The death rate for middle-aged persons is higher in the United States than in any other country in the world, despite our unexcelled medical and hospital care.* This rate may be associated with unprecedented prosperity. Some believe we eat ourselves to death. It may also be associated with the anxiety accompanying status striving. There is clinical evidence for both observations. Overweight is linked specifically with high mortality figures during middle age. Poor nutrition and poorer self-discipline are important factors. On the other hand, the need for a well-balanced life, with sufficient time given to family, play, and recreation, is also indicated by research findings, which long ago established a conclusion that those who exercise consistently have superior vascular tissue. Even if the middle-aged person himself has no cardiac accident or disabling disease, he has friends who keel over or are hospitalized. Whether overtly stated or repressed, many middle-aged persons are hypochondriacs, and these reactions spill over into marriage.

All this makes it difficult for the middle-aged to accept their real age. They often express attitudes which are conditioned by a sense of the shortness of life. They dislike to attend funerals for their friends because each death tolls the bell of fate for themselves. With decreasing energy, inescapable evidences of aging, increasing disability, and climbing death rate, it is really not unusual that some people in

---

*In addition to the factors mentioned in the text, one other not-so-relevant one should be added. The high death rate of Americans in their fifties and sixties is partially due to the fact that in any other country some of these mid-life casualties would have died in infancy or childhood. We keep many individuals with marginal health potentials alive in this country who, with less care, would not have survived. Thus this statistic, while seemingly negative, is really a tribute to life maintenance in our nation and a triumph for medical science.

their prime find it hard to be oriented to the future. Some of them jump at any chance for momentary physical pleasure or thrill. This awareness adds to their sense of bitterness about a mate they feel has inhibited them or shadowed their joy. Like the patients in my office, they feel that they have nothing to live for in the future, and this glum attitude becomes part of the cause of illness.

People like Bill and Helen have infinitely better health than their parents had at their age. Middle-aged men today can look forward on the average to three more years of life than their grandfathers could, and women to seven extra years over their grandmothers. More importantly, they will feel better, see better, hear better, and have more mobility during those years than any similar group before them. If they have the imagination to discover new vistas and sounds to excite them, they will also have more time to enjoy this extension of life. Grandfather worked, on the average, fifty-five hours a week, but his grandson works only thirty-eight hours, and this is destined to diminish. While the middle-aged person in 1900 had as his share of total national power for production but 1,000 horsepower hours of energy to supply him with goods and services, his counterpart today has 4,500. Consequently his income has doubled. The average income per person in 1900 was $800; today in equivalent dollars it is over $1,600, and careful estimates predict that it will double again by 1975. (While some 77.5 per cent of all males over fourteen are employed, 96 per cent of those between forty-five and fifty-four are at work and 85 per cent of those between fifty-five and sixty-four are in the labor force. There is much work to be done, and it is well rewarded.)

MAKING THE MIDDLE YEARS INTO THE PRIME OF LIFE

Today's middle-aged man has the whole world in his arms. Even these statistics give no real clue to his affluence. He has wings on his heels, wings to carry him to the seven wonders of the world. If he doesn't care to travel, the press, radio, movies, and television give him telescopic sight in his own den, so that no remote corner of the world is strange to him. All the culture of ancient and con-temporary worlds is his, either in accessible museums or on the silver screen. He can hear the folk songs of the shepherds or the crash of the Beethoven's symphonies at whim. He has the means, the mobility, and the time to thrill to the record performances of the world's greatest athletes, to laugh with the funniest comedians, or to cry with the most talented actors. And he does all this with fewer physical handicaps than any other generation that ever lived. He looks at the news from Africa and listens to the symphony with more discernment and appreciation than his forebears had because he has had, on the average, a superlative education. His children, too, are healthier, and he will raise almost all of them to maturity. At the same time he can be enjoying comradeship with a wife whose training and ability go far beyond curing hams and canning corn. All this infers another way of looking at the middle-aged. It is helpful to analyze carefully what those in the prime of life face in the way of problems, but it is even more valuable to look at what they can become. These possibilities are well summarized by C. Hartley Grattan, a noted adult educator:

> When John Walker Powell selected the three C's—Curiosity, Creativeness and Comprehension—as a basic to adult education, he also defined a trinity peculiarly meaningful to persons who have reached their personal resources, interests and prospects. This is the time of life at which all three can be given freer play than ever before, not encumbered by considerations of vocational training nor limited by the sense of inexperience which normally afflicts youth.[3]

Robert J. Havighurst, of the University of Chicago, has stressed the same general theme, that middle age is a time when one can re-design his life, take up new roles and alter old ones. He also suggests in terms somewhat different than Grattan's that the future lies with those who learn to value wisdom rather than physical energy.[4] One may quarrel a little with this demand that the middle-aged shift from physical pleasure to intellectual contemplation. Surely it is possible to develop "the three C's" and with them wisdom, but also to keep a healthy emphasis on sexual fulfillment and recreational balance. Then those in their middle years might embrace fully all the excitement of intellectual pursuit and aesthetic enrichment, and still have time and energy for physical activity. We would also add one other avenue for self-expression, the exploration of compassionate and critically needed participation in service activities.

It has already been hinted that the intellectual world for modern man has no horizon. To live in that world meaningfully, one has to develop a new wisdom. It is estimated that human knowledge doubled once from the dawn of conscience to the year 1600; it doubled again by the year 1900, again by 1950, and in the ten years between 1950 and 1960 it doubled again. As much insight and novel thought occurred in those ten years as in all of human history before 1950. Unless the middle-aged person keeps up, he will find that this "explosion of knowledge" has rendered him obsolescent and made him painfully aware of his anachronism. His mental tools were designed for another age, and his work attitudes were formed when there were no "systems." The middle-aged man watches the younger man deal casually with computer technology, building systems which he does not fully understand. Though the older man's record is impeccable and his loyalty unquestioned, his competence for this age is in question. For many, the dawn of electronic thought and automation is hung with clouds of panic or resignation. As these developmental processes invade more and more of industry, education, and space, more and more of those trained with slide rule and pencil are being shunted aside. It is no comfort that computer technology will eventually create more jobs than it displaces, because these new positions will go to those skilled in modern technology. Those in middle age are particularly susceptible to the demoralizing aspects of their obsolescence. The generation following has already been oriented to a new thought process, but even for them the choice of whether to study or not, whether to think or not, is no longer an open alternative. From this decade on, it is possible that the rapidity of invention and accumulation of research will mean that those who wish to excel can never leave the halls of learning. Is it impossible for the middle-aged man to catch up?

More than improving the middle-aged person's facility at work is involved in Grattan's emphasis on a renewed attention to creativity at mid-life. When children are raised and the early thrill and challenge of vocation dulled, the middle-aged man and woman are ready for another aspect of the life career. Their reactions to their "reassessments" differs. Some simply retreat from strenuous years of competition to the "idiot box." Others seek increasing oblivion through alcohol. As we have seen, others try for adolescent excitement in new romantic affairs. But there are others who recognize the positive potentialities of their next twenty-five years. They begin to pursue sculpture, painting, music, hobbies, golf, trips, sociology, religion, or politics. They renew interest by broadening the scope of their vision and their minds. They have determined to stay even with history and in tune with their times. They know that change and innovation are the hallmarks of this decade, that invention is now routine, and that the unexpected is commonplace. They are citizens of the late twentieth century and it does not daunt them. For them life is a daily adventure; but for the others every change is a catastrophe.

How men and women resolve the crisis of middle age is in a sense an indication of how they will live in retirement. If they do not perfect the use of leisure at this time, they will hardly be ready for a total life of leisure at fifty-five, sixty, or sixty-five. Middle age is a school for retirement, and new activities developed then bloom fully in the later years. Thus the positive adoption of new patterns in the middle years not only enriches those months, but also prepares the person for the last part of the life cycle. There are other aspects of this preparation that must occupy the attention of men and women at the prime of life, such as careful economic planning for the years ahead and conservation of health so that there will be some reserves to help enjoy retirement. When the problems of middle age are solved, it is hoped that in the solution will be a promise for a many-faceted life of satisfaction during the sunset years.

SUMMARY

If we summarize what we have said in this introductory chapter we can outline the pivotal tasks of middle age. These tasks form the outline for this book:

1. psychological adjustment to the loss of parental role;
2. achievement of a new type of independent friendship with married children;
3. acceptance and cultivation of the essential role of grandparents;

4. extension of the network of friendships and organizational contacts to make up for loss of intimacy with child launching;
5. successful coping with the fact of the male and female physical and psychological climacteric changes;
6. making sexual pleasure consonant with levels of energy and libido;
7. conservation of energy and cultivation of appropriate health habits in a well-balanced budget of exercise, hobbies, and interests;
8. expansion of intellectual interests with an upward reach to keep in touch with change;
9. development of a life pattern that will form the foundation for successful retirement.

2

Remembrance
of
Things
Past

No particular segment of family life can be adequately understood unless it is viewed as a product of the past interactions of all members of the family. It is obvious that much happened to Bill and Helen in their early married life and that much of this affected their relationship in their middle years. Chapter 1 focused on the mid-years of life, the years between the ages of forty and sixty; in this chapter we will try to look at all the experiences of the family as they affect adjustment during middle age.

The need to view family interaction as a whole in order to understand middle-age adjustment is seen clearly in the situation where the last child has left home and the couple are alone together. To understand how they adjust to this, we have to know what has happened to the marriage while the children were there and what experience they had with each other before the children arrived. If that early period before the birth of children was so troublesome that they have no positive recollections, they may react to the empty nest with dread. If, for instance, their early adjustment was so difficult that they had on a Friday evening talked about divorce and then discovered on Monday that the wife was pregnant and so decided to stay married, they may have little basis in previous experience for happily tackling a new period of being alone again. So all of life is bound together and no single period is understandable unless related to the total life experience of both the husband and the wife.

When Bill was talking to me about his relationship to Helen he said, "I really don't fathom what happened to us. Why don't we mean more to each other than we do?" Part of the explanation for Bill depended on his awareness of what kind of person he was and another part depended on his realization of what had happened to them as a couple. Middle age represents a great confrontation and a crisis point because the need for more intensive sharing tests both an individual's capacity to relate and the history of the couple's past efforts to relate.

Each stage in our lives has specific challenges which enable us to grow in relationship with others and to extend our minds. Each stage confronts us with special developmental tasks. Robert J. Havighurst has defined a developmental task as one

> . . . which arises at or about a certain period in the life of an individual, successful achievement of which leads to his happiness and to success with later tasks, while failure leads to unhappiness in the individual, disapproval by society, and difficult with later tasks.[1]

In this chapter we shall discuss the following stages of personality growth as they relate to middle-age adjustment:

Stage 1: Infancy and Childhood (birth–13)
Stage 2: Teen-age (13–18)
Stage 3: Courtship and Early Marital Adjustment (19–21)
Stage 4: Child-Bearing Years (21–30)
Stage 5: Child-Rearing Years (30–40)
Stage 6: Child Launching and Middle Age (40–60)
Stage 7: The Mature Years (60–70)
Stage 8: Old Age (70–death)

If we were dealing with child psychology we would separate the first period into infancy and childhood, but in the context of relating these periods to middle age they can profitably be combined. We shall look very briefly at the developmental tasks associated with each period and then show how each stage is related to middle age. A task for us in later chapters, based somewhat on the information given in this chapter, will be to see how the generations relate to each other, how the middle-aged person can find some contact with teen-agers and again with oldsters. In this chapter we are dealing more specifically with the past and future of the middle-aged individual as these determine his adjustment.

INFANCY AND CHILDHOOD

If we look back on Bill's and Helen's experience we can profitably ask whether or not there were influences during infancy and childhood which help to explain their dilemma in middle age. Lee Travis, a psychologist from the University of Southern California, and Dorothy Baruch, late and beloved child guidance expert, answered this question well:

> We have all lived through those long dark problems of childhood. Each and every one of us remembers at least in small proportion. . . . We remember also, how we were handled when these problems were upon us. We remember injustices. We remember righteous anger. We remember fury in return for fury. Penance, shame, regret. We remember what we did; what was done to us; what that did to us in turn—at least what it did to us at the moment. But almost never do we realize what it did to us for all time.[2]

Middle age is certainly a part of "all time," and we can profitably explore some of the crucial experiences of this early age.

The developmental tasks of infancy and childhood can be summed up in the phrase "growing up"—not in the sense of height, but in the sense of becoming human and humane. We take for granted the elemental tasks of weaning, toilet training, dressing, and developing habits. These are sooner or later mastered. The more difficult tasks of achieving sexual identification, developing a conscience, learning to communicate, moving toward trust and faith in others are not always so easily mastered. Blocks in these areas plague the individual the rest of his life.

Thus the way Bill's mother held him in her arms as a very small infant, with fear, with frustration, with some resentment, all became part of Bill. Her own sexual inhibition, reflected in the way she shamed Bill during toilet training, became part of his problem in accepting his sexuality and communicating tenderness. The fact that his father was not a strong male, that he did not give Bill enough time to learn masculinity, became part of his timidity as a male. The impatience of both father and mother when Bill had trouble with mathematics in school, their lack of response when he eagerly asked questions, was inevitably reflected in his problems of communicating with his friends and his wife. His sense of masculinity, his communication facility, a certain lack of trust and closeness were already part of Bill by the time he reached adolescence and the dating stage. These things were done to him for "all time," and are important in understanding the problems in touching and talking between Bill and Helen. We all have to build on what we are. What we are is partially if not largely determined by our experiences in infancy and childhood.

THE TEEN-AGE YEARS

The teen-age years are as pivotal as earlier experiences but built on them. These years in our society are devoted to becoming an adult. The adolescent in a sense experiments with various attitudes and values. It is a time when a person is neither child nor adult but caught. In my book *Education for Marriage,* I describe this period as follows:

In America, the adolescent lives in a tumultuous ambivalence. He feels new inner sexual tensions which discharge themselves in emotional outbursts or are dispelled through channels of high religious moral idealism. The adolescent struggles with the new sensations from within even as he tries to adjust to new and vacillating expectations from without. For now he is expected to conform to adult behavior patterns for which he has no background of experience. While his biological development demands growing independence of action, he often encounters the resistance of his parents who resent his repudiation of patterns of control which marked his childhood relations with them. The outcome of these years of struggle is decisive for marriage.[3]

This ambivalence is projected in a society with strident insistence on achievement in school and later in occupation and in marriage.

So almost every adolescent is beset with anxiety as he fumbles his way to some meaningful identity.

The developmental tasks of adolescence revolve around the selection of an occupation, preparation for choice of mate and later marriage, achieving poise and confidence in heterosexual relationships, learning to control impulsivity and emotions, accepting and enjoying the physical changes in one's body, and integrating a sense of values and goals that will guide and motivate throughout life.

Let us concentrate on the growth of heterosexuality and the integration of values as this relates to wise marriage choice, because these developmental tasks are most significant for our adjustment in marriage during middle age. If we follow Bill and Helen from childhood into adolescence and their dating life, we can discover growth patterns significant to every middle-aged man or woman.

Both Bill and Helen came from homes dominated by rejecting parents. They were not sure of themselves. They were awkward in social relationships and restrained in sharing verbally. Helen describes what happened to them during their high school days:

> Bill and I seemed to be just average kids, maybe a little shy. We were happy when we found each other because neither of us were too popular; not many boys had asked me out. It seems to me now that because we couldn't talk much, we spent too much time necking and petting . . . but then neither of us had had much love at home and we were both hungry for some affection.

They did not face the tasks of growing into competent adults because they were too crippled from their childhood experiences. They went steady all through high school and during as much college as they finished because, being insecure, they could not risk the competition of others. So they were not challenged to adjust to different personalities and different circumstances. They solved the individual tasks of this period by substituting dependence on each other for the dependence they had had on their parents. They avoided the tasks of achieving social and emotional maturity by relying too much on each other. Their development of poise and security in heterosexual relationships was limited to getting along with just one person. We shall see when we analyze the next period of their lives how this interfered with wise marriage choice.

During middle age their failure to grow during adolescence was reflected in a poor facility of communication, an inadequate sexual life, fear of intimacy or closeness to others, and a deep resentment of the dependency they had felt all these years for each other. They interpreted that dependency as a block to creativity, to autonomy, and to joy. Their relationship had remained on an adolescent level, and they both resented the life they had had and each other. If a task of the teen-age years is to try out various types of life attitudes and possible mates, the individuals inhibited by earlier experiences must surely be handicapped and develop frustrations that may come to the fore during middle age. On the other hand those young people who have a free spirit, who are not trammeled by parental fear, enter enthusiastically into all sorts of life trials and dating situations which help them sort out the type of life and mate best suited for them. If in a real sense we can speak of the middle-age period as a second adolescence (and I think we can), then the failures of the first period will ground the second in tumult and ambivalence.

COURTSHIP AND EARLY ADULTHOOD

Dating during the teen years inevitably helps an individual move into the later period of courtship and marriage—unless of course an unhappy home, emotional problems, sexual involvement or other factors have resulted in a teen-age marriage. Teen-age marriages have a desultory record in both early adulthood and middle age. Paul Glick, who works in the Census Bureau, showed statistically, in an analysis of 1960 census data, how tragic these marriages are:

> The proportion of remarried women whose initial marriage had occurred when the woman was below the age of 18 was three times as high as for women whose first marital venture came between ages 22 and 24 years.[4]

Harvey and Jane are a couple who illustrate what may happen when a poor choice is made on the basis of escape into marriage. This couple came to my clinic in their mid-forties to relate this story. They had married when he was eighteen and she was seventeen, largely as a matter of getting away from intolerable home situations. They did not realize their motivation then, but four years later, when they were a three-child family, they came to deplore their lack of courtship. They had not dated anyone else, and they had missed the fun and games of later adolescence. They separated for a year and tried to recapture their youth. But it didn't work because both of them had too many feelings of responsibilities about their children. They re-established their poor marriage, but without any outside help that might have enabled them to make a new start. Each of them was hostile towards the other, and the period of child raising was one of either indifferent tolerance or open battles. As soon as their last child was in high school, they determined to end the farce that had been their marriage. As a last effort they came to the clinic to see if, in their middle forties, they could salvage their marriage.

The developmental tasks of courtship and early adulthood focus on the choice of mate, the choice of occupation, and a final structuring of life's values and goals. Included in this period are those years of academic preparation for a career, the many months of pursuit by the female of the male she wishes to catch her, and the final emergence of solid character traits and life goals. Resolving all these tasks positively is crucial for success in all the later cycles of life. The following vignette of a case shows how conflicting values and marital problems are related.

Ben and Mildred had a long engagement period and waited to marry until she was twenty-one and he was twenty-two. Ben shared with Mildred his dreams of becoming financially independent by the time he was forty years old. Mildred found much satisfaction in his drive, as it seemed to answer her need for financial security, a security she had not known because her father was an alcoholic. The reassurance she needed at this point was so great that she did not reflect that the very drive she cherished might also bring her severe problems later on in their relationship. They were married, and both of them went to work to provide the base Ben needed on which to begin to build his independence. During the first three years they were happy and Mildred did not mind working, as Ben assured her that this was only her contribution to the affluence he was going to bring to her later.

All went well until at twenty-four Mildred became pregnant. When she radiantly announced this to Ben, he castigated her for her enthusiasm and insisted that she have an abortion. His lack of concern for her feelings as well as his moral outlook on abortion shocked Mildred. Ben insisted that they had agreed that they would have a large home, new cars, and many trips before they began their family. Mildred did not want the abortion, but Ben insisted and finally she consented but with great guilt feelings, which eventually turned to hatred of Ben. Furthermore, he was so engrossed in his goal of success that he neglected her sorrow and her needs.

Ten years later, when he had achieved substantial status, he proudly announced that they would now have their family. But it was too late. Whether for psychological reasons or simply the fact that Mildred had a low fertility index we do not know, but she did not get pregnant. She haunted the infertility clinics, but to no avail. This denial of her great goal in life left her bitter and aggressive. She would not come to a counseling session, but Ben related this melancholy story to me. She divorced him in her early forties.

One is reminded when one hears such records of marriage of what a very wise man said long ago: What does it profit a man to gain the whole world and lose his soul? Middle-age divorce, which is growing in numbers and percentages, often reflects the failure of the relationship during days of courtship and the failure of the couple to consider carefully all the factors that make a couple well-married. In looking at middle-age failures of love in marriage, we have to make some estimate of how adequate the beginnings were. Many middle-age problems are courtship problems which, because they have never been solved, mature in a final bitterness.

There is another series of events during the last stage of adolescence or early adulthood which holds profound significance for middle-age adjustment. It is at this stage that we resolve our values and determine our life goals and objectives. This is a period of self-idealism, and we look into the future as far as we can see and set very definite objectives. We determine what kind of occupational achievement we want, where we will live, the kind of mate who will meet our needs, our goals for our children. If those goals were always consonant with our ability, the middle years would not be so difficult. But in our time society puts such a high premium on economic rewards that many people aspire to levels of status and wealth that are not commensurate with their native endowment. The result is that at middle age we often have to come to terms with relative failure. Why this particular assessment is made during middle age is an interesting problem, but it probably has to do with a sense individuals have that the turning point in life is upon them. There is little doubt that the years from forty to sixty are years of evaluation. James Slotkin, a clinical psychologist, in summarizing case material divided life into periods and said that early middle life is ". . . the testing stage—beginning at about 43, when we start to reflect on our lives to determine whether we have achieved our goal, and to wonder if things have turned out as we had planned."[5] The individual compares his level of achievement with the expectations he formed during late adolescence. (We will discuss later both the way individuals cope with their sense of failure and a positive suggestion for dealing with this problem of second adolescence.)

The first years of marriage are those commonly thought of as a time of early adjustment, and this stage is terminated when children arrive. Less sanguine writers have called it the disillusionment period, and others have spoken about it as the time of the surprises. If a great deal of overselling has occurred during courtship or the couple have clouded reality by romantic idealization, they may have severe problems when the fact of marital intimacy discloses the real selves to each other. But even if the courtship was long and the engagement period functioned as an effective test period, couples are due for some dislocations in marriage. They may have known each other well as courtship partners, but this role differs from that of a partner in marriage. Marriage is an undefined situation for any single person. It is impossible to predict how any person will react to the closeness and new functional demands of marriage. Consequently this early marital period demands maximum flexibility and patience while the permanent habit patterns of the marriage are being solidified.

Decisions made during this period are apt to last throughout the couple's lifetime. The developmental tasks for a couple during this period are the refinements of their communication facilities in terms of problem-solving, decision-making, and need-meeting responses. They must finally merge their individual goals to create a unity of purpose and direction in their relationship. They must each make some compromises in individual attention to personal interests so that the concerns of the other are also fulfilled. In solving the problems of agreement and satisfying relationships early in marriage, the couple are not only making temporary decisions; they are structuring the whole future basis of the way they will relate during the rest of their married life. If the man prevails over his wife's desires by threats of force or if she gets her way by tears (what Alfred Adler, early German psychiatrist, long ago called "running a house by waterpower"), seeds of dissension are already sown that will come to flower sooner or later in bitterness and possibly a divorce. For each succeeding year will add an increment of dissatisfaction until at middle life, the accretion of frustration and sorrow may have built such alienation of one from the other that each will look at the other as an indifferent stranger when the last child leaves the home.

THE CHILD-BEARING YEARS

It may seem odd to some that we set the limits of child bearing as between twenty-one and twenty-six. But the average age of marriage today is twenty for women and twenty-two for men. And the average age of mothers when they bear their last child is twenty-six; this has been the case for over a decade.

The developmental tasks associated with the child-bearing years focus on the shift from the marital relationship to the family. As each child arrives, considerations regarding his health, comfort, security, and education loom large for both husband and wife. A new sense of responsibility is added to both. A further task is to maintain the physical and psychological closeness between mates that characterized their union before the coming of the child. Frequently adjustment to a larger family involves moving away from an apartment and into a home. The wife who has been working has to give up her work, at least for several months, and the family has to adjust its economic plans, for there is frequently less income but additional expense. One aspect of the problem is that often the coming of children alienates the father. The case vignette which follows illustrates some of these difficulties and how they affected a middle-age decision to divorce.

Harry was forty-eight and Eloise was forty-six when they came in to describe growing detachment and alienation from each other. I picked up a clue to the initial aspects of the problem when, in going back to their earlier relationships. Harry focused on the child-bearing years:

> No, we had few problems during our engagement and during our early marriage. I guess that was part of the difficulty. We were just too happy because when Eloise had her first baby everything fell apart. . . . What do I mean, fell apart? Well, I didn't exist after that. She had adored me before that but she forgot all about me. If I was too loud I was warned not to wake the baby. If I wanted her to go to a party she couldn't because the baby wasn't feeling well. Our sex life went all to hell.

Eloise had her side too:

> That's his idea. He wouldn't touch the babies, but he wanted them. Once they got here they were all mine. Besides he was playing footsie with his secretary while I sat home with a sick baby.

To which Harry responded:

> That didn't happen until it was obvious there wasn't any affection left for me here.

And so it went on—with increasing animosity—as they described an increasing gulf between them. In a conference recently a therapist remarked that he didn't know a case of middle-age divorce where the alienation had not started with the birth of the first child, the displacement of the father, his acting out in resentment, and the beginning of a long series of conflicts and tensions. He was exaggerating for effect, but the recitation given above is frequently repeated.

Harry did say one thing that was different. He suggested that when the relationship has been very complete the coming of the child can have more shock, particularly to a narcissistic person like himself, who really wanted a wife and children as jewels on his crown and, to change the metaphor, as servants in his cortege of loving admirers. It is obvious even from the few phrases of description given that Harry and Eloise had few real bonds in their marriage, that the euphoria or supreme happiness they experienced during their first years of marriage was bought at the expense of flying from reality so that the first real experience which tested them was a disaster. Modern women almost uniformly describe their first years of motherhood as the most difficult in their lives; especially at that time they need the utmost in understanding and devotion. If it is not forthcoming they may, as Eloise did, withdraw from the husband and seek consolation from the children.

The case also reveals a characteristic of some husbands who declare the nursery off limits to themselves until the children are capable of some independence. Fathers are parents too, and any denial of this by either the husband or the wife makes gross difficulties for the marriage and for the children too. A father who will never take a turn at the 2 A.M. feeding, regardless of his wife's fatigue or do the dishes when she is knee deep in diapers or bottles is asserting a strange type of masculinity. How deeply this hurts was reflected by one mother who said with sorrow about this period, "Dad deserted us for eight years."

THE PERIOD OF CHILD REARING

This period is thought to extend from the time the last child becomes mobile until the last child is an adolescent. We date it uncertainly from ages twenty-six to thirty-five years, but there is much overlap. By now the warp in the family design is evident. A good counselor can predict quite well what will happen to the rest of the marriage on the basis of what has occurred up to this date. What happens during these years is very likely to reflect and amplify the modes of interaction established previously.

The developmental tasks of the family during this period center, sometimes too exclusively, around the growing needs of the children. As the years pass their demands become more costly, both in money and in time. In the middle-class home Mother is often frazzled by the multiple tasks confronting her—as chauffeur who provides transportation to a dozen organizations and an infinite variety of lessons (tennis, swimming, dancing, etc.), as home teacher, as PTA member, community organizer and canvasser, wife, cook, and sometimes business partner. Father is straining now towards whatever aspirations he has in his occupation and matching his advances against the increasing financial demands of his family for their current and future needs.

Mother often plays her family role to the hilt, seemingly unaware that when her children reach high school a life career devoted exclusively to them will terminate. If, at the same time, her husband is devoting most of his energy to his work, their communication becomes meager indeed. The widening separation promises disaster when child launching comes and husband and wife are left literally to each other.

On the other hand, to be fair to the majority of parents we should also say that many experience this as a period of profound satisfaction. The frequently tiresome and irksome period of early dependency of childhood has passed. Something of the uniqueness and promise of each child is appearing. The boys are content and enthusiastic to go with Dad to a ball game or play football in the backyard, and the girls are already showing the first signs of feminine interests. If the children have had some freedom, they are excited now at each new discovery; they often come from school with discoveries of ever-broadening horizons of information and concepts. They are old enough to climb a mountain, run in the surf, and bait a hook on vacation. Each day is an adventure for parents who have such children. If the parents have maintained the primacy of their relationship so that each step in occupational growth by the husband is interpreted to mean more life for the family and not increasing isolation, that family grows in cohesion and devotion. If, again, the family economy is well planned and each child is growing in responsibility for a part of the family chores, Mother's long period of servitude is modified and she has more energy to enjoy both the children and her husband.

We should not forget either the large number of women who go back to work during this period. In the average home the last child has entered kindergarten by the time the mother is thirty. And while the number of women working reaches its low point at this age, this is also the point at which it begins to go up again.[6] It continues to increase until age forty-eight, and does not reach the lowest point (where it was at age twenty-nine) until age sixty. An increasing number of women are working during the period of child rearing. We have already hinted that their adjustment problems at middle age are essentially different from those of women who find their entire satisfaction in child rearing.

CHILD LAUNCHING AND MIDDLE AGE

This period of the family cycle sometimes is part of middle age, depending on when the last child was born. Furthermore it is difficult to decide when a child is really launched in our society. Many fifteen- and sixteen-year-olds are so independent and hostile to their parents that they have virtually no relationships left with them. Many other young people can be said to be "launched" when they get married, enter college, go into military service, or take a job. The aura of excitement and pleasure surrounding a marriage or entry into college is such that the separation is clothed in drama and its significance for the life at home obscured. In the average American home the last child is born when the mother is twenty-six, which means that he is college age (eighteen) when she is forty-four. Of course this varies because age twenty-six is the mean; it may be much earlier for some and considerably later for others.

The developmental tasks of child launching are twofold. Whether the child is going to college or into marriage, he must be sent away with ceremony and proper equipment. For college this means a period of shopping for clothes, luggage, and writing equipment. For marriage it means the hope chest, showers, and wedding preparations. In either case it is interesting that in the United States, where the rites of passage into adolescence are often minimal, there are rituals that attend child launching. These events have the manifest function of simply preparing the one who is leaving for his or her future, but they have a more hidden function in helping the ones staying home over a difficult transition.

The transition only begins when Mother and Father put the last

boy on the airplane for a distant school or stand on the church
steps and wave a final good-bye to their radiant youngest daughter.
Their next days of behavior are veiled to their friends, but often
both parents wander about the home and look at mementos from
an exhilarating past—and try to remember how these rooms, now
so still, used to echo with rock and roll, loud laughter, or singing.
Although they are somewhat comforted to know that their newly
marrieds have promised to visit and that their boy will be back for
vacation, they are aware that they won't ever really be home again.
All the daily tasks taken for granted all these years are suddenly
laid aside, the responsibilities, often worrisome, are now relayed
to others' shoulders, and the constant dynamo of adolescent activity
is abruptly stilled.

Child launching is one of the great crises of life for both the
father and the mother. We have already described in some detail
the trauma it introduces, and we will not repeat what has been
already said. It is important, however, to see this event in the long
history of family life in order to realize its challenge. It is only one
of many transitions that mark middle age, but it is a major one.

As the total emphasis of the remainder of this book is on meeting these tasks, it is inappropriate even to summarize such efforts
here. However, it does seem critical, before we move on to make
positive suggestions, that we vary the presentation a little and consider the question of what means for dealing with these tasks are
at the disposal of the middle-aged person. Is he truly at the prime
of life or is he already on such a decline that his lower intellectual
and social abilities are themselves responsible for much of his middle-age stress? This is an important question and we turn to research for an answer.

One of the most extensive and careful studies of personality in
middle and later life has been done by Bernice Neugarten, head
of Committee on Human Development, University of Chicago.[7] In
one basic aspect of her Kansas City studies she raised the question,
What importance does age have in accounting for problems of mental health and adaptability of those from age forty through sixty-
five?

The investigators for this phase of her study (Robert F. Peck and

Howard Berkowitz) used a long interview together with several cards from a projective psychological test to study differences between people at different age levels in several basic areas of personality adjustment; namely, flexibility in the ability to invest strong feelings in new activities and experiences; flexibility in the ability of mental processes in solving new problems; the growth of many diverse areas of life to give satisfaction to the self rather than to depend on one or two; the ability to use one's body well and to enjoy life despite whatever difficulties one might have with poor health; the capacity to be freed somewhat from egocentric concerns and give some of oneself to others; satisfaction with one's body itself; and the capacity to mesh one's sexual desires with other aspects of life. Finally the researchers constructed a way of measuring general satisfaction which they called *adjustment,* or the effectiveness with which an individual was adapting to his life situation. A most significant result of this study was the conclusion that none of these eight measures vary much because of age.

Neugarten says: "The lack of age differences—especially the lack of a downward trend in adaptability with increasing age—suggests that aging, per se, at least between forty and sixty-five, does not result in decreasing mental or emotional flexibility."

The results of this study have two important consequences for us as we look at what can be done to make middle age a period of growth and satisfaction. The first is that all the tools are available and there is not general deterioration in either mental or emotional operations to account for any of our problems. The second consequence is a reaffirmation of our basic point in this chapter that whatever inability there is to meet the crises associated with the mid-years for any family is to be seen as a consequence of a longtime failure of the husband-wife relationship or of the poverty of the personality resources of one or both. Indeed Neugarten herself says something like this in reference to mental health:

> The finding strongly suggests that personality patterns are firmly established long before middle age and that they tend to continue throughout adult life . . . if good adjustment in middle age and old age is largely the product of emotional health and sound development in children, it is not only a measure of child welfare but also a measure for successful aging.

We would want to modify this statement in terms of the family somewhat and suggest that while optimum personality development contributes to wise marriage choice and good marital adjustment, marriage has its own crises, challenges, and history and that the outcomes in middle age are partially due to the way in which the problems have been structured.

LATE MATURITY

When we move beyond middle age to late maturity (ages sixty to seventy) our emphasis changes completely. While we have been attempting to account for some of the factors contributing to the marital problems of the mid-years by looking back on processes that resulted in those problems, we now change our focus and concentrate on the way our behavior and experience during these years prepare us for the next stage of the life cycle—namely, the stage of retirement. During this time the individual "concentrates on achieving the maximum gratification from what remains of a vigorous life."[8] His chief developmental task is to prepare well for retirement and then adjust to it. His wife's task is to help him prepare for it and then to adjust to him in retirement. We shall see how subtle this task is when we discuss ways of achieving future results in this field.

OLD AGE

We have designated old age as that period from age seventy to death. The termination point for the family is the death of one of the partners. The developmental task for those in old age is to utilize their remaining years in intellectual and aesthetic ways so that each year brings new satisfactions and pleasures. As the man of middle age looks toward the sunset of life, he will want to prepare for it economically, so that he will have sufficient resources to avoid financial desperation, and intellectually and culturally, so that he will have a background against which to enjoy his life when he must turn increasingly to mental rather than physical pleasures.

One of the problems the middle-aged person faces is his relationship to his own aging parents who have become less than competent to handle their affairs. This creates a dependency on their part on their child or children and results in an inversion of the previous authority patterns. Ways of understanding and handling these patterns will be discussed in Chapter 6.

SUMMARY

The focus of our introductory chapter was to see with some clarity the essential nature of the problems and opportunities that are inevitable in middle age. In this chapter we have tried to understand this period as it is the product of the past and the anticipation of the future. Life is a river in time, and while it flows around bends and becomes deeper and more calm in places, it carries with it both the force that comes from its past and debris it has accumulated with each mile traversed. It would be possible to treat middle age by itself without looking intensively at how it achieved its configurations and color, but to do so would lose for us its reality. Even now we have achieved some insight into some of the reasons for family failure during these years and this background will stand us in good stead as we look intensively at the particular difficulties already outlined.

3

Roles in the Family Team

When we watch a second baseman, we know that his duties on the field are different from those of the pitcher. He has to cover second base in case there is a double play. On the other hand, he is stationed far to the right of the second base bag in order to prevent a well-hit ball from bounding through that territory. He likewise must catch fly balls that are close to the infield. There is a whole cluster of duties that he assumes as soon as he agrees to play that position. These are his functions and every position on the baseball field has different assignments.

ROLES AND ROLE PLAYING

In the United States today it is quite popular to call these clusters of duties associated with any position "roles." Because these duties are functions associated with any position, we call them "functional roles." Every man and woman has many positions. For instance, that second baseman is also a father, and on returning home after the game assumes a great many roles by that position. During the off-season the second baseman may work as a salesman in a broker-age house selling stocks and bonds. He now has a third status and a new list of roles. Every human being's life is made up of statuses or positions and associated roles. They define his behavior, his obliga-tions, and his identity.

If we think carefully about roles, we recognize that some are more important than others and some involve directing the role playing of others. Thus the captain of the team may tell the second baseman to move a little more to his right because he knows that a particular batter has a tendency to hit to that spot. If there is an argument between the players, the captain may make a decision on the spot, which all the other players are expected to follow. However, if the argument concerns something that is very vital, he has an obligation to stop the game, take time out, and confer with the manager of the ball club because the manager's role is to make all the important decisions. If we then put on a chart the relative power and influence of the people on the baseball field we would say that the ballboy makes almost no decision, the second baseman makes many deci-sions but they are often at the specific direction of the captain, who in turn is following directions from the manager. Each role then has two aspects: It includes the tasks assigned to the person who plays that role, but it also includes an understanding of the degree of autonomy and the degree of initiative deemed proper for that posi-tion. This aspect of role behavior is called "control roles."

In order for a team to play smoothly and the players to win, each team member must feel a degree of responsibility for doing his task well and for performing it in the way he has been instructed. No baseball team would ever win if the players were completely auton-omous and doing whatever they decided themselves was proper. No business could function at all unless the secretaries, salesmen, sales managers, vice-presidents, and executive boards felt some compul-sion to perform their tasks according to the rules defining their posi-tions. Society as a whole has defined many of the rules in our society. Thus a man in our country may not marry five wives. The role of husband is defined so that it involves supporting, defending, and loving only one woman—at a time. (Dr. David Mace, former execu-tive director of the American Association of Marriage Counselors, in commenting on the high divorce rate suggests that America is moving to serial polygamy—many wives, but one at a time.) These rules that go with a role are often regarded as quite sacred, and constitute the morality of the community. The rules are learned along with roles. A normal human being feels profound compulsion, as he accepts any role, to obey the rules and to play the role well.

When a boy or girl is growing up, he or she observes the way Father and Mother play roles. The child identifies with the functions he must perform, with the rules that are associated with the role, and learns the level of power that goes with the role. The growing child and adolescent soon learns that all adults around him *expect* that if he grows up to play second base or be a husband, he will behave in certain carefully defined ways. Thus these "expectations" determine for any person his behavior. If he does not live up to the expectations, he may be dismissed from any position. Any group must demand that its members behave according to expectations or else it would be in chaos.

Society makes it possible to have order and cooperation in human endeavors by developing common expectations around significant roles. This applies to the family as well as to all other human institutions. Things go smoothly when both husband and wife *perceive* their mates' expectations accurately and behave accordingly. But if a wife does not perceive the way in which her husband believes a wife should behave, she may disturb him greatly by doing things that he thinks are wrong for a wife to do. Or, if she *perceives* accurately what he wants her to do as a wife but does not herself share that expectation and does the opposite because she thinks it is right, she may also disturb him greatly. Trouble in marriage can come partly because one partner does not communicate his expectations to the other, but it comes as frequently because of disagreement about the manner in which the role of wife (or husband) is going to be played.

ROLE CHANGES AT CHILD LAUNCHING

Roles change during the period right after child launching to such an extent that both their functions and their control aspects undergo radical transformation. How these are settled determines much of the future of the couple. There is some proof of this in a study done in Cuyahoga County, Ohio, by Marvin Sussman, Professor at Western Reserve University.[1] Particularly interested in social role changes in middle age, Sussman took a random sample from a list of twelve thousand marriages recorded during 1956 and traced the parents of the couples. This gave him a group of middle-aged persons. He wanted representatives of both working- and middle-class families and persons who were between the ages of forty-five and sixty.

Sussman also wanted to know how much continuing relationship there was between his subjects and their married child's family; since that information will be valuable for us in a later chapter, we will record it here. He studied this continuity by measuring feelings about the child's marriage, feelings about the child-in-law, closeness of the family, how often the children came for advice and used it, what happened to the family celebrations, the extent of visiting between parents and children, communication between the generations, and help given to children after their marriage. His conclusion was that there was high continuity for families of the low social class, but the higher the social class the lower the continuity. He went on to say that this did not mean that previous findings of continuity for the middle class were to be rejected, but that more study should be done.

To study the impact of middle age on role behavior, he studied the way eleven social roles were performed after the departure of the last married child. After the interviewers had determined what behavior, such as giving help, had been before the child left home, they then asked about the types of help given since the children's leave-taking. In four of the eleven social roles (the roles of parent, spouse, user of leisure time, and church member) more than 50 per cent of the couples reported changes since the leave-taking of the last married child.

A higher proportion of those with little family continuity reported that there had been intensified interaction between husband and wife after the last child's leave-taking. Couples reported spending more time together and more mutual activity. Middle- and upper-class men and women said that most of the changes had occurred earlier for them, at the time their children had left home for college rather than at their children's marriages. We have already suggested this possibility in the last chapter. The researchers found, too, that the higher the social class the more the couple's use of leisure time changed after the children were gone. The lower the interaction of parents with married sons and daughters the more active the parents became in church work.

It is obvious that with child leaving there is a large block of time and energy that has to be redirected. The couples interviewed in Sussman's study expanded their reading, games at home, trips, driving out, hobbies, course taking, television viewing, and sports. The middle and upper classes spent less time with their married children and more with their friends than the lower social classes. It was found also that the married children of these higher income groups were more mobile than those of the lower income group and that fewer of them were living in the same area as their parents.

After the children left home, their father's role as worker did not change in type of work, but rather in degree of commitment; the fathers were working harder than ever before. Mothers experienced great changes in their tasks of meal planning, housekeeping, and shopping. They had more time for themselves and their husbands. Sussman's study establishes for us the significance of role change at middle age; the complications it brings will be our next question.

We can find something of an answer to the question of the meaning role change has for middle-aged husbands and wives in a significant study by Robert O. Blood, Jr., and Donald M. Wolfe.[2] These two research professors from the University of Michigan gathered information from a group of interviews with 731 urban and suburban wives and with 178 farm wives. The interviewees were chosen from a sample of families in Detroit and surrounding countryside. The study was carefully done and the analysis of the data is very competent so that we can rely on the conclusions reached.

Blood and Wolfe developed a scale to measure the degree of power which the husband and the wife exert in their marriage. They refined their study so that they measured the degree of dominance by the husband and by the wife through different stages in the life cycle. From their data we can see what happens in middle age. We can discover if the wife, now freed from the cares and concerns of child raising, uses the time and energy to increase her power role in relationship to her husband. If she moves in this direction and the husband has less and less power, this might account for Sussman's observation that the husband during this time tends to become more alienated from home and to intensify his work role.

This very simple table from Blood and Wolfe's study provides us with such insight that it is worth a good look:

TABLE I

Husband's Power, By Stage in the Family-Life Cycle[3]

Stages in the Family-Life Cycle	Husband's Power[*]
Honeymoon	5.35
Preschool	5.71
Preadolescent	5.41
Adolescent	5.06
Postparental	4.79
Retired	4.44

[*]The numbers here are derived from a scale (0–6) which measured relative power of husband and wife.

It is obvious from this table that the husband's strength and the wife's dependency are greatest when the children are being born and reared. A wife does not have time or energy for much contact with others so that her dependency increases. But when the children are launched at the beginning of middle age the wife grows in power for decision making and influence. Blood and Wolfe comment that "In any case, middle age appears to be a time of peak wife-domination in Detroit (as in Kansas City according to Neugarten, 1956). Women in their forties and fifties appear to achieve a strength and self-confidence which younger women seldom know."

They also make a significant comment which adds to our analysis of contemporary marriage at any stage of the life cycle. They say that the "dead hand" of a patriarchal past is gone and that the application of power in the contemporary family is made in terms of the "individual skills in particular areas of competence." The patterns of decision making vary, depending on the individual's abilities to contribute, and this enhances the general competence of marriages.

CHANGING ROLE PATTERNS AND THE NEED FOR COMPANIONSHIP

If the thesis is correct that both men and women now share decision making and allocate tasks on the basis of ability, we should then find that there is a new *division of labor* in the American home, that the traditional male and female roles are being increasingly shared by couples. Indeed this is the case. While lawn mowing, snow shoveling, and household repair are still tasks of the male and dishwashing, straightening up the house, and cooking still occupy the wife, other tasks are now more equally shared. According to Blood and Wolfe's study, paying the bills and keeping track of the money is always done by the husband 19 per cent of the time, by husband and wife equally 34 per cent of the time and always by the wife 30 per cent of the time. But role specialization tends to increase year by year so that by the time the children are launched the husband and wife *do fewer and fewer* things together.

Shared decision making not only indicates a couple's respect for each other but also involves considerable time in companionship. We would thus expect that the greater number of decisions shared, the greater would be the wife's satisfaction in her companionship with her husband. This turns out to be the case. Where the wife shares only two or fewer decisions her average satisfaction score is 3.68 on a scale Blood and Wolfe developed; when she shares three to five decisions her average satisfaction score is 3.96; and when she shares six to eight important decisions her satisfaction score increases to 4.26. At any stage of the life cycle *companionship* seems critical to the satisfaction of the wife.

If companionship is critical to the wife, we would predict that that group of husbands who are upwardly mobile and who "intensify" their concern for economic success during the middle age would have dissatisfied wives. Blood and Wolfe found that this was true:

Such neglect seems to be especially common among success-oriented husbands (the same husbands who are least available to help around the house with household tasks). . . . Similarly, high income husbands especially in the $7,000–$10,000 bracket, have conspicuously dissatisfied wives. Apparently these husbands are so tied up with their occupations that they are too busy both for housework and for leisure time companionship.[5]

The most profound needs that are involved in companionship are those for tenderness, for emotional support, for contributions from the mates for emotional well-being. We have already indicated that when the wife loses her role as mother she has no one to turn to but her husband. A wife's great need for emotional support is one of the crises of her middle years, and it is important for us to stress this point as we discuss role change in middle age. We are assuming that an American wife has few emotional resources outside her immediate home. Her parents are now old, infirm, and often far away. Her own brothers and sisters have migrated to other cities. The accuracy of this analysis can be seen when we realize that during the child-bearing stage of marriage, when presumably a young wife's mother and father are still around as sources of emotional support, she still depends on her husband almost 50 per cent of the time to always share their problems. But as wives become more mature, reliance on the husband gradually decreases. They are either alienated or emancipated from him by middle age. The couple's talking with each other is at its lowest ebb. They "drift toward silence."

What is the wife's general satisfaction at middle age with the marriage in which she is assuming more power, in which there is less emotional support and less interaction as a couple? In terms of the wife's love for her husband, Blood and Wolfe comment that "Length of marriage and number of children combine to leave mothers in the launching stage seldom enthusiastic and often bitter about the loss of the husband's affection and companionship."[6]

For many couples there is renewed companionship, and this is a period when the husband gives more time and attention to his wife. Nevertheless her satisfaction with love is considerably lower than it was during the honeymoon, preschool, or preadolescent phases of the family cycle. It will grow still lower during the retirement period. Wives' general satisfaction with the marriage declines with every decade. Time is a *corrosive influence*. Blood and Wolfe showed that while something over half of the wives are very satisfied with their marriages during the first two years, twenty years later (at middle age) only 6 per cent are still very satisfied and 21 per cent are "conspicuously dissatisfied." The marriages have disintegrated. Husband and wife no longer talk as much, interact as much, or do as much for each other. They find satisfactions in their work, in their friends, sometimes in their children but *seldom* in each other.

This loss of satisfaction with marriage gives an explanation of middle-age divorce and the growing incidence of family disintegration in the forties and the fifties. Blood and Wolfe conclude their study by asserting that the "deepened habituation through the years" is enough to keep the couples together despite alienation and the loss of satisfaction in the middle years. This would seem to be a counsel of despair. Blood and Wolfe tell us that as life's end approaches, one wife in four is still enthusiastic and another one in four is still quite satisfied; what they don't say is appalling—that one half of them are not satisfied with what remains. The pivotal conclusion of Blood and Wolfe's study is this: that the estrangement which occurs during the child-rearing years is often permanent, so that for the rest of their lives husband and wife "live . . . as relative strangers under the same roof, searching elsewhere for companionship or being resigned to a life of increasing loneliness." Is this result inevitable?

ALTERNATIVES TO ALIENATION

There is an alternative. Half of the middle-aged couples studied are destined for loneliness and increasing alienation, but the other half found another way. It is the remarkable providence of human beings that they are not inevitably driven by either circumstances or instincts to follow blindly a course of despair. Every middle-aged couple has the opportunity for a second honeymoon followed by increasing intimacy and the resurgence of interaction and communication. Consider the case of John and Jean.

John came home just four months after their last daughter had gone off to college and found Jean crying; Jean had had high hopes for the time when their children were gone. She has always wanted to write and had set off for a junior college in her area and enrolled in a writing class. She had many friends her age that she liked, and she was determined to renew relationships with them. She bravely told John that she was going to take golf lessons so that one day a week she hoped to play golf with him. None of this had materialized very well. Her English teacher was not enthusiastic about her short stories; her friends had their own lives and their own problems; her golf drives curled out into the rough. She recognized that all of these plans were not very substantial anyway. She had too much time alone and there was no sound in the house. But beyond that there was a void in her emotional life which neither writing, nor friends, nor golf would fill. She became more and more depressed, and finally could not conceal it from her husband.

When John heard her sobbing in their bedroom he climbed up the steps two at a time, took her in his arms, and comforted her. Then he patiently asked her to tell him what was wrong. As the story of her failure to adjust came out, he was patient and understanding. The next day he called his office and said he would not be in to work that day. It was springtime, and although he lived in a semi-desert area in California, he knew where the spring creeks were swollen and flowers blooming. He drove Jean there and they walked by the creek and recalled how the flowers had been in the Midwest in the springtime. That weekend he canceled his golf game with his regular foursome and, instead, took Jean to a driving range and helped her with her bad drive. Afterwards they went out to a restaurant and danced. On Sunday they stayed home, had a late breakfast together, and spent the day talking—and planning for the years to come. Jean's depression was gone.

Her depression was gone, but something else took its place. When John stayed home and then gave her his weekend, it was not the time with him alone that was important. It was his understanding of her feelings that buoyed her up. It was his attitude that neither his work nor his friends were as important to him as she that gave her the answer she needed. So of course she responded with deeper tenderness, and John was struck by what he had missed during the preceding years in their growing alienation. Together they planned each month to include more and more things both had secretly wanted to do but which had not been possible when the children were around. I knew them well because they talked with me with

a profound conviction that they wanted their next twenty years to
be the most rewarding of their lives.

And it was. I see them now and then, but not too often. They
are too busy as a couple crowding companionship and adventure
into their lives to either need or want to spend much time in a
counselor's office. Each year their Christmas letter gaily recounts
new adventures and new satisfactions. Five things seemed to account for the new spirit in their lives:

1. They have achieved a *new intimacy*. They replaced their deep
but secret longing for closeness with each other with open decla-
rations of devotion. They proved their words of love with little
demonstrations of concern. For instance they began to call each
other on the phone in the middle of the day—a practice they had
given up fifteen years before. They learned to reserve one part of
the day and of the week when nothing else mattered but their sharing with each other. They learned that planning a weekend was
almost as much fun as going. Instead of growing "silence" they
learned how to laugh, and to love, and to play. Above all, they re-
established the sense of tenderness which had been theirs at first
during courtship and the honeymoon, and they always said it meant
more now—because now it was very real, while at first it had been
a little play acting.

2. They learned to *intermingle their roles*. Aware that part of
the chasm that had grown between them came because of their
sharp division of labor, they consciously began to modify the formula
"This I do and that you do." John took to drying the dishes so that
Jean could be through with the after-dinner chores earlier and they
could have more of the evening together. Jean took over paying
some of the bills, a task John had always done, which freed John
from some laborious night bookkeeping. They learned to work together in the yard and even to plan the spring planting together.
While John cut the yard, Jean trimmed. Somehow this worked so
that they always had time for nine holes of golf or an afternoon drive
along the beach. The important thing, however, was not what they
did but that they grew in their ability to plan together in such a

way that they both agreed on their leisure-time activities and organizational interests. There was no covert struggle between them over power. Jean did not follow the rule of "peak dominance" during these years. They both followed the rule of never being satisfied with a decision unless it meant a real consensus which pleased them both.

3. They developed a *deeper relationship with friends*. Some of their friends had moved away and others still had children at home, so they decided that in addition to these they needed to cultivate closeness with some additional couples who were in their same stage of life. John found some at work and Jean located some in her church acquaintances. They quite purposefully cultivated them until they had found a group of stimulating friends who were in the same situation as themselves. These new friends could go with them on weekends or on an evening. These couples also needed to replace some of the emotional investment they had previously given to their children, and welcomed John and Jean into their lives with real enthusiasm.

4. They achieved a *new relationship with their children*. When their son and daughter had found mates and been married, they had seemed to reject too much intimacy with John and Jean, and this had hurt the parents. But after John and Jean talked it over and remembered the needs they had had as newlyweds to establish a new home and a new closeness, they wisely withdrew for a time and waited for their children to invite them. When they came together they were very careful not to give advice, not to criticize, not to take sides, and not to give any evidence of jealousy or dissatisfaction. They concentrated on making the evenings with their married children full of laughter and praise. After some months one of the young couples showed up asking for advice. The parents tried to talk over the problem as adult to adult, and the young couple were most grateful for their insight and for their attitude. After the relationship shifted from that of parent–child to friend–friend, it remained so for fifteen years. While business took the young couples far away they still write often and make every opportunity

to see each other whenever possible. This transition was possible because Jean found her emotional needs satisfied by John, and no longer had to turn to her children for love and tenderness or for satisfaction of her feminine needs to be wanted and to serve.

5. They developed new and broader *avenues of service*. Another reason Jean could realize a mature relationship with her married children was because she was satisfying her need to be wanted through social service. Even as a girl in her own home Jean had been the one who had helped her younger sisters and brother. She had a profound need to be nurturing to others, and as a mother this need had been adequately met. When the children left she found some opportunity to serve her husband, but this did not wholly exhaust her energies. John suggested one day that a speaker at his Kiwanis Club had mentioned his work on the board of the Spastic Children's School in the community, and expressed their need for volunteers. At first Jean did not think she should try such service because she feared that she would react with too much emotion to little children with handicaps. Later she decided to visit the school. Its principal introduced her to some of the older children who had been there some time and who were able to dance, write, and study. Jean's heart went out to them, and soon she was working there two days a week. Her capacity for patient understanding fitted her for the work and she did well. In fact she did so well that she soon had John on the board raising money for the school. They both found a permanent and rewarding interest in this effort. Inevitably this service introduced them to many other types of social service, and they became active in leadership training and volunteer recruitment in the community. While they worked together in these projects, they never became so embroiled in so many activities that their own relationship was jeopardized. They grew closer and closer as the years passed.

SUMMARY

Both research studies and case histories indicate that there must be a redefinition of role during the critical years of middle age if marriages are not to be sterile, silent, and dissatisfied. If the wife persists in her motherhood role, she will alienate her married children and disrupt her relationship with them. If she persists in carrying on roles that are effectively alienated from her husband, the chasm between herself and her spouse will be broadened. If her husband is a busy businessman, and does not modify his concentration on his work role, he will lose the possibility of meeting his wife's needs during this time. Evidently half of the marriages under study fail to meet this crisis, but half of them succeed in re-establishing closeness and harmony.

The case of John and Jean has indicated that it is possible for couples to arrest the process of alienation and to find new and satisfying roles. Analysis of the experiences of this couple indicates that five shifts in role expectations and behavior helped them achieve a new life together. These were: (1) a modification of their emotional roles so that they found new intimacy and response; (2) a new way of performing their functional roles—the tasks they carried on—so that they worked, played, and planned together; (3) a new role with friends, who became much more intimate parts of their lives as they explored new ways of relating to others; (4) a new role in relationship to their children so that they shifted from being parents to being friends and companions with those children; and (5) learning to play a new role in the community by investing some of their time and energy in service to others. It is obvious that the achievement of these transitions only occurred with a great deal of talking, planning, and awareness. Adjustment to any of the family life cycle crises does not happen automatically. It is the result of honest assessment, evaluation, and the willingness to invest time and energy for each other.

However, such an achievement on the part of any couple may be almost impossible if either the husband or the wife is having inner battles over his or her identity. If the husband is locked in the inner struggle over his awareness of middle age and approaching old age, it may be impossible for him to be sensitive to his wife's needs. What we have suggested in this chapter as essential role shifts depend on both the husband's and the wife's resolution of their own personal middle-age crises. For that reason our next chapter concentrates on an analysis of the resolution of the problems of male and female identity during middle age.

4

Identity Crises at Middle Age

There is a time in the life of every person when he is filled with exaltation at being. It may be that this awareness comes when, as a lad perched on a limb of a tree, he is wondrously aware that he as a self exists. Or this surge of self-consciousness may come later after a tender hour of devotion with his young love. Sometimes it comes even later, in a class where the teacher shares with him the eternal wonder at being. This poignant moment of discovery of himself in a vast and seemingly timeless universe changes his view of self forever, because he now is aware. Sooner or later he asks of himself and about himself, "Who am I? What is my relationship to all this about me that is not me?" To finally know oneself as a unique individual, to accept that self as worthy, and then to share that worthy uniqueness with others is all part of the task of discovering and developing one's identity.

THE SEARCH FOR MEANING

The long struggle of childhood and adolescence is concerned with the honing of the self to make it acceptable and with facilitating the ease with which that self communicates with others and establishes a distinctive place in the world. A hundred years ago religion contributed a solid framework that reinforced both the sense of self and the rules for relationship with all that is not self. But at a time when religious authority is fragmented into a thousand voices, one does not so easily find a sense of belonging through religion. Science gives us physical comfort and new lenses to look for truth but, by definition, confines itself to limited questions that yield equally limited answers to the man wanting to know who he is and if there is anything in the universe that cherishes him.

The answer for many in our time is to forget the search for meaning in life by substituting things and comfort. Some limited affirmation of self is possible in the drive for things, because if one can accumulate enough of these, others will praise him. The one who drives the Cadillac and lives in the house on the hill has visibility and envy, even if he has no sense of purpose other than owning more Cadillacs and bigger houses. But the competition for things brings its own anxiety and, often, its own mediocrity. And if one is to be successful in the market, he has to deny individuality, to conform, to be bland. Any expression of an individual's feeling for social justice that would disturb others, any deep feeling of emotion, any prophetic insight impairs his position in the competition. So, as David Riesman of Harvard University says, men become like weather vanes, with only the most sensitive radar to detect almost automatically the attitudes of others and respond like robots to them. The self becomes an anxious mirror of others; the quest for meaning of the self is lost in mass obeisance.

It is questionable that the personality package which sells optimally in the marriage or the commercial market is really enough for lifelong satisfaction as a mate. Playing the "pleasing game" with all the skill one can muster leaves the questions of meaning unanswered and the individual lonely and afraid. There are other diversions for the self that is afraid—in sex, alcohol, and drugs—but all of those eventually lead to satiation and, finally, to boredom and illness. The mass man's contacts must be superficial, lest he disturb others or raise questions that are frightening to himself. As a consequence, his needs—the deepest ones—for intimacy and belonging find no response. True, every individual sees more people than ever before. Leaving a football game or making a shopping tour, he may be immersed in waves of humanity, but every other individual is an indifferent stranger. There is no encounter. He comes close enough to others to present no problem to the pickpocket, but no one picks the lock of his heart. He is so close to others that by necessity he absorbs the germs of another's cold, but so far that he cannot feel the warmth of a single human smile. In the home, where our own anxiety in the competition is translated into anxiety that our children be adequately trained to compete, little energy is left for tenderness and almost no time for the long and patient explorations of questions of identity or destiny. Furthermore, the quest for things is a restless one and eternally mobile, prohibiting anything more than the most shallow contacts with others. There are people, but few friends.

The very environment seems destined to promote the image of self as only another cipher on a vast, impersonal social computer. The self finds no hills upon which to gaze for strength; he is destined to fight his way through the grey concrete canyons where millions sit in the cubicles which make up that computer and respond when the machine selects their number. He is as powerless as the machine on which he audits the day's profits to change the system that engulfs him. But he is anxiously alert to the signals from the system that cue him in his effort to move to a larger cubicle and a larger machine. He eagerly gives extra effort to such opportunities as training courses or sensitivity seminars that will help him conform more smoothly and move more quickly into the bigger room with its greater anxieties. But his alertness and energy are so exhausted by this rat race that he has no time for contemplation or the expansion of inner self. As I have said in another place, "Small wonder that half of our hospital beds are filled with those who could not stand the smoke, the tension, the bustle, the nervous derelicts burned out by the friction of such an accelerated and frequently unlovely life."

It is no wonder that man, denying his uniqueness by being a cipher, does not often use his unique self as a committed and involved citizen of his community. The contradictions of our society may vaguely trouble him, but he denies his responsibility for them and wishes they would go away. If he has any sensitivity at all, he may view with chagrin the gulf between our Hebraic-Christian norm of forgiveness, compassion, and peace and our almost continuous destruction and mass death but, except for annoyance at those who insist he think about that problem, he can dismiss it as beyond his understanding or influence. He may have some moments of confusion at the contradiction between our continuous affirmation of freedom for the individual and the wholesale denial of that freedom to vast minorities, but if there is the slightest chance that Negroes will move close to his symbol of status (his home) he quickly resolves his feelings. The fact that we can double and then double again our gross national product in one generation and still leave a very large sector of our society without homes, medical care, or education may make him wonder, but only until he gets his tax bill. So man is alienated from that part of himself which stands for justice and for ideals.

The individual is also deeply alienated from others who are not comfortable with such a denial of problems. He is angered because increasingly youth are so shocked by these contradictions that they "drop out." Recently when more Harvard graduates opted for the Peace Corps than for a place in corporations, their fathers raised a righteous and indignant protest that echoed across the country. In some cases such actions by youth invigorate old guilts on the part of parents who at some cost had cut their own involvement. In other cases such action threatens the parents and all other members of the Establishment by questioning the ultimate values they live by. If nothing else the dropouts and the Peace Corps electors highlight the inadequacy of contemporary structures to give identity and meaning to individuals. The fact that in every city in the nation divorce, drug addiction, delinquency, and crime attest to the inadequacy of human interaction and strength of self is lost to the parents because they do not think about meaning.

THE CONFRONTATION OF MIDDLE AGE

The search for identity reaches its highest pitch during middle age. There are a number of reasons why this is so. Men and women at the midpoint in life are like the Roman god Janus, who had two faces, one facing backward and the other forward. This period is unique in that, in a sense, it represents a second adolescence. Both men and women between the ages of forty and sixty seem compelled to rethink their lives, to reassess their goals, to ponder their achievements, and to plot the course that will be theirs in their remaining years. With a limited number of months ahead, with evidence of physical decline inescapable in every step and every look in the mirror, they can no longer avoid making some judgments about their worth in the past and their prospects for tomorrow. Many are poverty-stricken in this effort, for in an other-directed world there is little habit of contemplation and few mental or spiritual tools developed for such a task. Not having much personal identity, and often having been unwilling to get involved in social efforts that might have given some sense of worth, they find their individuality is shattered. Furthermore, many middle-aged persons have worshiped so long at the shrine of youth that they have no sense at all of the dignity and value of maturity, so that their middle-aged evaluation is often only a visit to the wailing wall rather than an assessment of new goals and new values that would be available for the later years. It is for this reason that many men, being both unable and unwilling to face aging, intensify their work habits; they seek to avoid the confrontation of self by such absorption in occupational effort that they have no time or energy to ask or answer questions.

Yet such a confrontation cannot forever be forgotten or denied, says the psychiatrist Edmund Bergler; he believes that every man must sooner or later face the implication of aging. Bergler defines the situation almost exclusively in psychological terms and emphasizes the problems that result in sexual and personality conflicts. Our frame of reference is larger, for the sociological and spiritual aspects of this crisis seem to be equally significant, if not more so; poverty of self before forty intensifies identity crisis for both men and women after forty. In a sense, the middle-age crisis of identity is but the culmination of all the efforts and failures in identity formation throughout all the previous years. Furthermore, the resolution of identity problems at this divide in life probably determines the positive or negative way in which the role problems discussed in the last chapter are resolved. If an individual is completely involved in his own private struggle over his self-concept, this inner conflict interferes with his ability to attend to the needs of his mate or of the changing marriage. Let us look in on a couple where this occurred.

Mike and Jacqueline had had a relatively productive marital relationship until their late forties. Their last child had left home to make a good marriage, and Jacqueline considered child raising a task well finished. While she missed the children, she was a little fatigued and was perfectly willing to turn the rest of her energy in the coming years to her husband. But he rebuffed her. He withdrew into long periods of silence and was annoyed if she interrupted his reading or his television watching. While he did not say much, she felt that his voice was flatter, and sometimes had a tinge of melancholy.

Occasionally he telephoned her, with some irritation, to say that he had to work later than usual. Several times he was unusually late, but gave no explanations. After a year in which the silences grew and Mike seemed to become somewhat sloppy about his dress, speech, and work habits, Jacqueline demanded that they talk. For several months she marshaled all of her tenderness and patience in an effort to understand what was happening to her mate. Mike insisted at first that he missed the children. Later he stated that he had lost all enthusiasm for his work. When she asked him about their sexual life, he became very angry and accused her of lacking understanding. When nothing that Mike said made any sense, Jacqueline made an appointment for them with a marriage counselor.

The marriage counselor was responsive to Mike's description of his plateau at work and his sense of loss of the children. He worked very hard on these areas, and Mike got up enough courage to ask his employer for a change in what he was doing. The employer gave him a different type of work with some new incentives. Mike was encouraged by the counselor to renew a limited relationship with his married children, which he tried. He followed all the prescriptions, but remained depressed and withdrawn. The counselor asked for some individual interviews after Mike had burst out in one of the sessions with "It's a rotten world!"

In the individual interviews Mike began to talk about his world and its people. He had grown up in a small town in the Midwest where there had been a good deal of openness and friendship. In San Francisco, where he now lived, relationships seemed to him to be casual and on the surface. He longed for the intimate comradeship he had shared with the boys on his block throughout adolescence. He and his wife had some friends their age, but their interests seemed to Mike to be superficial. He had to force himself to continue to see them. But he maintained that there was no difference between their value systems and his own.

It seemed to the counselor that Mike insisted on the last point too vehemently. What did he believe? During the following few weeks Mike recited a rather consistent string of middle-class platitudes. The counselor asked him about his youth. Mike described his high school and college days when he had been a debater. He had grown up during the depression, and he once explored the luxury of being rather radical for those days. But, he said, he had learned the danger of this when he lost his first job because at that time he had been too vocal about the promise of labor unions. At the mention of labor unions he showed more emotion than at any other point. He was almost manic as he denounced the power grabs and the exorbitant demands of contemporary labor. He moved from labor unions to the government and gave an embittered analysis of "creeping socialism." He was on the point of moving into an equally severe indictment of the "civil rights" people when the hour was up.

In the next few weeks he revealed that his son, who was now in college, was exploring "radical" ideas as he himself once had. He grumbled about the fact that each generation had to make its own mistakes, but he hoped that one day his boy would see the light. When he was asked if it were better that his boy and others be idealistic even if naïve, he somewhat changed in mood. He told about the time the college president had called him on the carpet and he had stood up for his convictions. After that recollection he was silent a long time. He finally faced the counselor and blurted out, "It's easy for us to forget those days." It took Mike a long time to uncover the cost to his integrity and his imagination of "playing the pleasing game." In the process he had chained his sense of justice, his alert mind, and his individuality in order to conform. He said he had traded his "convictions for comfort," but he really had no comfort. He had given up involvement and denied the guilt he felt about it, but the guilt was there. After some months his depression was gone and he began to function again, but on a much broader plane that had relevancy to problems of society. A most relevant comment has been made about men like Mike by an architect and planner in Los Angeles, Frank Hotchkiss. Mr. Hotchkiss was given a sabbatical by his company and asked to write a report on his thinking during the period when he was away from work. Surprisingly, much of what he had to say in that report was not about city planning but about the men of our cities:

> The middle-aged, who have the skill and energy and capability to do the most, often shy from the real tasks, deny their imagination and intuition, and settle for dreary compromise. It is the hectic, shortsighted striving of the middle-aged that is most filled with vanity and which too often constitutes the wasteland of our lives. Thus it appears that youth is not wasted on the young but rather that capability is wasted on the middle-aged.[1]

Mike had not directly confronted himself with his moral compromises and their crippling effect on his "imagination and intuition." Basic to his sense of himself as a male had always been his sense of physical maleness. He had prided himself on his physical prowess; it alarmed him when his doctor, at the conclusion of his annual checkup, advised him to modify some of his most strenuous activities. He had to confess during that checkup that he had experienced some impotence in his sexual relationships with his wife. His doctor sensed the anxiety of this and responded to that anxiety by being casual and by indicating that at his age this was normal. But, normal or not, impotence threatened Mike and he began to be worried; he became intensely reflective and evaluative, and later depressed and withdrawn.

THE CRISIS OF MIDDLE-AGED MAN

What was happening to Mike physically? The male sex hormone, androgen, is manufactured by the adrenal cortex and by the testes. In addition a small amount of the female hormone, estrogen, is always produced by the male. This production peaks at age twenty, and this level, on the average, is maintained until the fifties. From then on, it decreases steadily until age eighty, when very little is produced. Its diminishing effect on the male has profound importance in determining mood and reaction. William H. Masters and M. D. Ballow, physicians, have called the period in which this occurs "the third stage of sex":

> The sex interest is retarded, and acute awareness of this may produce a chain of undesirable mental reactions. In their milder forms these are a lessened interest in life, loss of the usual "spring" in the intellect, diminished combativeness, and states of indecision over trivial problems.[2]

However, it must be remembered that the male change generally occurs later than the female so that except in singular cases, Masters and Ballow are describing a phenomenon that occurs generally late in middle age. Nevertheless they stress the fact that ". . . Many students of the subject believe that this gonadal aging process is accelerated in those leading restricted sex lives. There may be justice in this view, since disuse itself accelerates atrophy."

This evidence would account for the sexual panic on the part of middle-aged persons as afflicting those who (a) aged rather rapidly and (b) had not had a very active sexual life.

Isadore Rubin, editor of *Sexology*, has described in detail some of the changes that are significant as the result of lowering androgen levels.[3] The prostate gland begins to enlarge after age fifty, although serious growth may not occur until the sixties or seventies. The reason for this growth may be an imbalance between male and female hormones. The testes atrophy somewhat as they decrease in size and lose their firmness.

The cells in the testicles that produce sperm thicken, and sperm production slows. The ejaculation becomes scantier and thinner. A longer time interval in intercourse is required to reach orgasm. Fewer erections occur.

Three other doctors, Elmer Hess, Russel B. Roth, and Anthony F.

Kaminsky, stress the symptoms which, after fifty, may disturb the male.[4] They speak about the diminution of libido, hot flashes, sweats, generalized weakness, loss of mental drive and energy, poor concentration, and emotional instability that characterize some male patients. In these cases they think it is proper to speak about a male climacteric as comparable to the female involutional period. They are careful to distinguish between "primary physiological" and "secondary psychosomatic" factors. These doctors think that the symptoms listed above may accurately be characterized as "instances of androgen insufficiency."

Rubin has described some of the other causes of impotency that are rooted in physiological conditions which may assail middle-aged men. Any serious illness that involves suffering or weakness results in lowering of sexual drive. Diabetes and thyroid disease may produce impotence in some men. Tranquilizers, sedatives, and narcotics vastly interfere with normal sexual response. As these are consumed in vast amounts by the middle-aged, it is probable that they do much mischief to the sexual lives of tense men and women. Dr. Magnus Hirschfeld and Dr. Donald Hastings, as reported by Rubin, think it is quite possible that excessive smoking may reduce potency. Rubin mentions other authorities who think that both impotency and excessive smoking are the result of high anxiety states and that there is no causal relationship between them. On the other hand, stopping smoking is not apt to reduce anxiety, so that return of potency, which both doctors report after cessation of smoking, could hardly be due to any shift in anxiety.

In addition to the inevitable decline in libido due to losses of androgen levels and to other more general physiological states, there is a further loss, due to the simple fact of anxiety over aging. The causes for much middle-age impotency must be located, not in organic changes, but in the emotional sphere. Dr. Donald Hastings, who is head of the School of Psychiatry at the University of Minnesota, has stressed the significance of the "fear of fear" phenomenon.

I remember one relatively young man, just reaching forty-five, who had become alarmed because he did not react to his wife with the same zest that he had in his twenties. To reassure himself of his potency, he had begun an affair with a secretary in his office who had been described by colleagues as an easy victory. He arranged his rendezvous with her with a great deal of secrecy and planning and with an equally high level of anxiety because he was afraid that if he failed with her he would know for sure that his life powers were waning. At the last moment he telephoned her and complained of a severe headache, but promised to make another date. He never did. Whenever he approached his wife, it was with growing alarm that he would not have an erection and often he did not. This was so painful to him that it caused his anxiety about himself to increase again to the point that he could not be potent at all.

This man had other evidences of middle age. He struggled unsuccessfully with temptation at the table and bought larger and larger belts. His hairline was receding so that he employed all manner of arrangement of what hair was left to cover the vacant areas. Although he had serious chest pains, he continued to play a violent game of handball. Much to his wife's disgust, he began to associate with much younger companions and to insist that they go to parties much more appropriate for those just married.

He went through five years of inner hell, during which time he came to blame his wife for all of his difficulties. While he had made a respectable living, his earnings fell far short of his adolescent dreams and he blamed this failure on her. That he could no longer be potent with her or try a relationship with other women he also regarded as her fault. So he became hostile and bitter to her and so alienated her that she could not cooperate in any effort he made to assure himself that he was not really an "old man." He reviewed in fantasy all of his earlier romantic expectations for his economic and his sexual life and found that now, with life nearly over, he had been cheated. He finally brought himself to the place where he could have an affair with a younger woman, but by this time he knew before he went to bed with the girl that he would fail. And fail he did. It was at this point that I saw him for the first time. He had no self-esteem left. He was in a typical identity crisis.

In the beginning of this man's difficulties with his wife fatigue played a significant role in reducing his libido. He came home from work burdened by the day's difficulties, worn out by worry, and anxious about what the next day would bring. The consequences of living in such a "chronic fatigue state" have been well described by Joseph Trainer, author and medical marriage counselor:

> The destructive element in this pattern is its unrelenting constancy, made necessary by the marginal economics that dictated the arrangement to begin with. Such people are fagged close to their daily limit and crown the physiologic limit with inadequate sleep. This is a true chronic effort fatigue status and it robs the individual of energy, without which there is no zest. No zest means no pleasure and no pleasure means a dull life, with a persistently trickling drain of resiliency.[5]

The consequences of this life with "no zest" have been powerfully described by a pioneering psychiatrist who wrote with insight and depth about sexual problems, Wilhelm Stekel, who related impotency to economic drives for status and power:

> The hypertrophic cultivation of the "will-to-power" has brought in its wake a situation wherein the majority of civilized men have neither time nor energy left for love . . . indeed, the accumulation of wealth may attract to itself all of the libido originally destined for love, and may again become a symbolic substitute for love, which again and again is demonstrated by well-marked examples of the miser. . . . Scant energy is left to be spent on love, but not withstanding, the demand for love is growing. . . . Half of all mankind is now suffering from this conflict between sexual want and sexual ability.[6]

The fuse for the process that characterizes the middle-aged man's crisis, then, is often set off by either a sense of sexual failure or by other physiological decrements. But in a very basic sense these signs are only the beginning of the process. They may signal to the person that he is at the divide, but they by no means describe all that is viewed from that point. His diminishing sexual powers, his declining vigor, his bodily and cosmetic changes give the alarm, but the profound crisis of the male self involves all that he wanted to be and all that he failed to be. The focal point may still be his commercial goals and the way he achieves them. But for most men their relationships with others and their social world will occasion most distress or reward in their "self" review. If a man has violated his inner ethical self, he must either rationalize this or pay the price of guilt and reconstruction. If he has completely succumbed to the "outer-directed" ethic, he will only be confused that the foundations of his inner self are crumbling and the absence of profound commitment, involvement, intimacy, and purpose will not be solved because they are not within his framework of reference. But whatever his situation, he is in an "identity crisis" that poignantly reflects both his individual past and the crisis of his society.

THE CRISIS OF MIDDLE-AGED WOMAN

The middle-age crisis of women in terms of identity seems much more specific than that of men. Many women have a very focused identity during their first forty years: they are the creators and sustainers of life. This fact has pervaded almost all of their actions and attitudes during these years. Unless they have invested a great deal of energy in work, they do not measure their identity by achievement outside the home. Most women who work do so to provide for very specific needs of their families, and in a very real sense that work is but another phase of their caring for their husbands and children. The career woman who regards child bearing as incidental and motherhood as only an interruption to her main role in life tends to have troubles in middle age similar to those of men. As the majority of women relate their careers to motherhood, we shall devote most of our attention to their identity problems.

There are very obvious signals to a woman that the meaning of life is changing at its midpoint. Her ovaries atrophy completely, her menstruation ceases, her capacity for ovulation and, consequently, for motherhood is inevitably terminated, and much that was her badge as a woman disappears. Helen Deutsch, a psychoanalyst, has said that the mastering of the psychological reactions to organic decline is one of the most difficult tasks of a woman's life.[7]

A forty-five-year-old woman wept her way through an hour in my office. Her doctor had told her that she was menopausal, and of course some of her weeping was due to endocrine imbalance, but not all of it. She said:

There's nothing left for me. I wanted eight babies. I wanted all I could have, but my husband said three and no more. I loved those babies. I loved their softness, their cuddling, and their cooing. I loved to pat them, diaper them, powder them. I sang to them and rocked them and played with them. They are all gone now and I can't have any more. Nothing matters anymore. I wanted to try last year once more, but Bill said No, we were too old.

Women enter what Deutsch calls a preclimacterium between forty and fifty. They often wish for a last baby during this period. This preparatory stage is marked by modified glandular function and often results in such physical symptoms as vasomotor disturbances, flushing, dizziness, headaches, and psychological states of insomnia, anxiety, excitability, and depression. Menstruation becomes irregular, and the woman becomes aware that she is beginning the "change." Deutsch described this period:

> With the approach of the climacterium, new motherhood is impossible, and the frustrated activity is directed toward other goals . . . at the moment when expulsion of ova from the ovary ceases, all organic processes devoted to the service of the species stop. Woman has ended her existence as bearer of future life, and has reached her natural end— her partial death—as servant of the species. She is now engaged in an active struggle against her decline.[8]

Women tend to move from the preclimacterium to the actual climacteric between forty-five and fifty-five years of age. Specific timing is related to the loss of ovarian hormones. The amount of estrogen and progesterone is reduced, which results in the loss of feminine traits. They no longer can balance the adrenal production of the male-related androgens. The breasts tend to sag, and the uterus diminishes in size. The skin loses much of its elasticity so that it tends to wrinkle and sag. The pattern of hair growth changes. The lining of the vagina and the labia thins. Vaginal secretions are generally scant. Quite gradually but inexorably the entire reproductive system becomes inactive and unnecessary.

The psychological losses that occur with the withering of the physiological functions vary considerably from woman to woman. For many women it is fair to say that "her beauty vanishes, and the warm, vital flow of feminine emotional life as well." The emotional responses are the most significant ones. Doctors estimate that only 40 per cent of women have any menopausal symptoms of a physical variety. A female facing her "partial death" responds in a variety of ways. A few women, like the middle-aged man, may resort to coquetry and seek to reassure themselves that they are still attractive by bold seduction of younger men. Others attempt to defend their self-esteem by almost manic behavior. They want their lives to be full and active. They join a great many community organizations, sign up for class after class, enroll for a higher degree at the university, and take golf lessons. Deutsch suggests that some women "behave like girls in puberty." They paint their faces and spend heavily at the dress shop "in order to have the illusion of being admired and loved." Still others withdraw into isolation to protect themselves against frustrations in seeking proof that others love them.

Of course there are many realistic women who do not need to deny the fact of the climacteric or escape it but who still react with some depression. The depressive reaction may be due to a temporary imbalance of hormones or it may be due to a realization that all of the significance of twenty-five years of meaningful activity has closed. Just at the time the woman is aware that she is changing physiologically, she is called upon to face a major role crisis. Up to this time she has occupied almost all of her hours as wife, mother, and housekeeper. Now most of that activity has little point. Her husband may or may not be happy with his accomplishments in his occupation, but in any case he will be focused on it. Her withering glands say to her that her major contribution is past, and the empty rooms in her house emphasize the message. As she becomes depressed, she may be subject to many fears for her health, her worthiness, and her future.

Some of the self-observations of Deutsch's patients suggest an identity crisis:

> Women who are good observers of themselves report that, confronted with the climacterium, they experienced a kind of depersonalization, a split, in which they feel simultaneously young and old: "Is this aging woman really myself? Only a short time ago I was that promising young girl, whom I feel in myself still so alive."[9]

Those patients are reporting almost the same feelings that mark the middle-age crisis in men. One looks back with longing at the zest and beauty he had in his early twenties instead of contemplating the decline in virility and beauty that is inevitable in old age. "Who am I now? What does the future hold?" These are monumental inquiries every woman has to face one way or another.

STEPS IN THE RESOLUTION OF THE FEMALE IDENTITY CRISIS

The crisis of identity comes for good reasons to both the husband and the wife. If this crisis cannot be resolved, the degree of egocentric concern and terror will certainly frustrate any effort to build new roles in the marriage. How can one deal with the need for a new definition of self-worth in this period? Deutsch came close to saying that there are few compensations, and that successful psychotherapy in the climacterium is made difficult because there is not much to offer the patient to replace fantasy gratifications. She says that at least for now, aging women must accept the status quo and wisely base their positive life values on what they can still enjoy. But Deutsch wrote in the mid-forties. A great many exciting physiologic and psychologic changes offer more hope than that for the contemporary woman.

While it is true that the whole reproductive tract and the vaginal vault are generally transformed due to the loss of estrogenic hormone with consequent irritation and even pain, these symptoms can be overcome without great effort. Many gynecologists are going beyond the recommendation of a simple lubricant to recommend local applications of estrogen in commercially prepared creams or suppositories, which not only seem to improve the elasticity of the tissues of the vaginal wall but also restore to some extent the vaginal lining. Much of the itching of the vulva that seems to follow the thinning out of the tissues disappears. This treatment relates only to the amelioration of local vaginal conditions.

Dr. Robert Wilson, of New York, has been widely quoted in both medical journals and popular women's magazines on the use of estrogens to alleviate symptoms associated with estrogen starvation. He thinks that the deprivation by nature of the source of health, well-being, and attractiveness can now be overcome by estrogen replacement. This treatment has already changed the careers of thousands of women, but some women do not need estrogen supplementation. The physician can easily determine to what degree a woman's body is producing a normal amount. When she has an adequate amount of hormone, menopausal distress is certainly due to emotional difficulties and no amount of physical treatment will cure her problems. There is some possibility that estrogen is coming to be regarded by a section of the population as another miracle drug that will settle all troubles of middle and old-age. Such a simple solution to the complexities of middle age is suspect.

There is a second problem which is associated with any discussion of estrogen therapy. It has been widely held that estrogen was associated with cancer. Some physicians thought that it caused cancer. Others thought that while it might not be a causal agent, it would intensify any cancerous growth that might be present but unsuspected. Research results do not conclusively establish the truth or error of either of these positions at the present time. Some insight has come to us about this because of the widespread use of contraceptive pills that contain hormones. It is interesting that a large foundation has recently presented one of the discoverers of the birth control pill with a large grant to study the influence of hormones in inhibiting cancer. The grant was given on the basis of findings that patients on the pill had developed a significantly lower rate of cancer than others not on the drug. Isadore Rubin reports that women whose ovaries have been removed have been found to have an incidence of heart disease seven or eight times that of a comparable group of healthy women. The results of current research, presented at a recent day-long scientific meeting on the effect of the pill on tissue abnormality, seemed to indicate that no such developments could be identified at the present time. Even so, we must say that the final verdict is still out on this matter. The research laboratories are investigating, and the very best thing a woman can do is follow the advice of a competent gynecologist who follows research closely. Nevertheless hundreds of thousands of women are, as Dr. Wilson says, aging more gracefully because of such treatment.

Doctors Masters and Ballow are quite convinced of the safety and value of hormonal treatment, provided that a desirable ratio of testosterone and estrogen are taken together, as this maintains the kind of balance essential to good health. They say that "there is usually an amazing resurgence of physical strength and mental awareness" in individuals who receive this kind of treatment and that "once a plateau of regenerative activity has been attained, continued steroid support will maintain this plateau indefinitely."[10]

A case history of a woman we will call Ellen is instructive. Ellen was forty-nine years old when she came to our clinic. She had been a highly productive writer for ten years, but due to depression and marital conflict, all of her creativity was gone. She made many attempts to substitute other activities, but her interest was short-lived, and only added to her sense of despair. Investigation revealed that her depression had begun about the time her last child left home. At the same time her husband had been promoted to a job that demanded more time, and she felt abandoned. All these seeming factors in her situation were investigated thoroughly. Joint conferences were held with her husband to try to improve communication and interaction, but nothing he did pleased her. She developed increasing irritability and hostility.

She had seen two different therapists before she came to our clinic. These men were competent therapists, but she had left them. When we explored her physical situation we discovered that she had been given sedatives and vitamins but that no one studied her endocrinological situation. Upon our insistence, she asked a gynecologist to run a series of tests to determine the level of her estrogenic hormone. It proved to be almost at the zero level. The gynecologist immediately put her on a consistent program of estrogen therapy. In succession she reported the following developments: (1) her depression lifted; (2) she found new interest in her writing and in other interests she had tried but abandoned; (3) her libido returned and she shyly told us that she had even awakened her husband because she "wanted him"; (4) she evidenced new zest and laughter; and (5) she discovered she did not need therapeutic intervention in her life anymore. Of course it is possible that the work in our clinic was just as important in her recovery as were the hormones, but I don't think so. While we are not deprecating the value of her counseling with the other therapists or with us, no change occurred until she was on an estrogenic regime. Then the recovery was dramatic and sustained. Probably the most significant observation that we made about this woman was that she regained her capacity to love life and her husband. The case indicates how important it is for any kind of therapeutic help to be based on competent medical support.

To love has always been the expressive function of women. It has many facets; only one of them is included in reproduction. A woman can be motherly to her own children after they have left home and to others in her environment regardless of her age. The menopause places no constriction on that ability unless the symptomatology is so severe that it brings emotional distress with it. The relationship most women have with their children moves from mother-as-authority to mother-as-friend when they leave home. She can also look forward to mothering her grandchildren if she treats her own children as adults. And she has many opportunities to give love to other children through social service.

These activities and interests probably will not be her only source of a new identity. She may find some job that will interest her and give her creativity a chance to blossom, but even a job may not allow her to invest enough of her emotional self. If she is to switch the concentration of her love from her children to a new love object, she will probably find the solution in richer relationships with her husband. That is exactly what we concluded in the last chapter when we were talking about her role. What new insight has been added? Precisely this: the suggestion that the solution for her individual problem of a sense of self-worth will not be found within herself but with her mate. If she understands the identity problems he is having with his inner self, she will be in a position of helping him. She will not be frustrated when his ego problems are so enormous that he cannot always respond to her needs. The solutions suggested for those problems in role discontinuity must be solved by better communication and more sharing between husband and wife, but the insights in this chapter can make the interaction possible.

STEPS IN THE RESOLUTION OF THE MALE IDENTITY CRISIS

What about the husband? Can he, too, look forward to testosterone replacement to modify the threats to his identity in the middle years? Testosterone treatment is not likely to be as effective or prescribed as generally for men as estrogen treatment is for women. One reason for this is that the male's middle-age distress is generated by social and psychological factors during this period to a greater degree than is his wife's. His so-called climacteric does not occur until later, if it occurs at all. The factors we have stressed—overwork, status drives and consequent fatigue, and a consequent loss of libido—are not apt to yield to any form of physical medicine. Another reason is that many physicians frankly label the administration of androgens as "dangerous business." In the article already cited by Drs. Hess, Roth, and Kaminsky, there is a review of several studies on the incidence of carcinomatous changes in the prostate of men over fifty. In reviewing studies they report that some 20 per cent of every one hundred patients probably have "symptomatic carcinoma of the prostate." They report that ". . . There is adequate clinical and experimental evidence to indicate that when a prostatic carcinoma is already present, the administration of androgens is likely to accelerate its growth and promote its spread."[11]

They then say that the use of a balanced androgen-estrogen complex (such as Masters and Ballow recommend) is not supported by experimental evidence. Furthermore, the relationship of the administration of sex hormones and their influence on sexual desire is still an object of dispute. There are "some conflicts in available evidence," and until more clinical evidence is presented, it is impossible to find any basis for recommendations one way or the other.

While there is little doubt that advancing years diminish the male's sexual capacity and while there is considerable doubt about the utility of male hormone treatment, recent studies indicate that neither of these factors are basic to dealing with the male's sexuality. Much evidence will be presented in the next chapter to indicate that sexual failure during middle age is largely psychosomatic. The average male can extend his sexual life far into old age if he so desires and if he promotes his general health. While signs of intermittent impotence may trigger the middle-age crisis, an existential difficulty is at the heart of that crisis, as has already been indicated.

We have defined the central focus of the male's identity crisis as his need to deal with the meaning of his life or his tendency to avoid confrontation with meaning at all. This implies that at the divide he must inevitably make an inventory. He has to study calmly and profoundly the payoffs of his previous years, their worthiness, and what those achievements have cost him. There is no way to escape a rigorous confrontation with self. While it is true a middle-aged man probably reviews the goals of his earlier years and totals up his record in achieving these goals, he must realize that twenty-five years ought to change perspective. What was dear then may seem later not to be so important. This is the mark of growth. Rather than lament lost years he ought to be grateful for an increment of wisdom which indicates that the years did not pass without gain.

SUMMARY

If in that critical analysis that seems to involve an assessment of identity, Mike and Jacqueline find that they have grown complacent to new challenges and impervious to new ideas, there are years ahead to change that posture. The libraries and bookstores are still open. If they find that their relationship is indeed shallow and they are restive because of lack of intimacy, they can still reach out with tenderness one to the other, who likewise may feel "like a stranger in our midst." If their marriage has all the aspects of disenchantment, a few months of attending to each other will bring new closeness and reward. If they have grown callous to injustice and if they are noninvolved with the future of their fellowmen, there are great causes in large and small endeavors all around them.

The pivotal behavior at the divide is commitment. The future of Mike and Jacqueline will be entirely different than for Bill and Helen or Mary and Jim, but as long as Mike and Jacqueline, Bill and Helen, Mary and Jim make it their own future with their own goals and express their own identity, they will grow in meaning and reward.

5

Sexual Success in the Mid-Years

SEXUALITY AS THE AFFIRMATION OF TENDERNESS

Sexual success in the mid-years is extraordinarily important for both men and women. It is important, not for the relief of the pent-up drives that characterize adolescence, but as a symbol of a union between two people who have learned to care deeply for each other. Its function in the mid-years is the affirmation of tenderness and the unspoken token of togetherness. By middle age the fires have been banked, but the glow and warmth of the fire is even more comforting than the tempestuous flames that consumed a couple in their earlier years. The physical union of a man and woman during this period is equally rewarding, but it is different.

It is this difference that every middle-aged man and woman needs to accept. There is some tendency in these days of the worship of the eighteen-year-old bunny and of youth to forget the increments that come with each age. Hugh Hefner's *Playboy* world is a very limited sphere. He has nothing to say to those whose love is long and rooted in the past. The bodies of the bunnies are indeed delightful, but we get little insight into their minds, their emotions, their experience. Yet it is upon the long interaction of mind, mood, and living that love develops. And it is in the rewards and commitments of love that security and contentment lie. We do not quarrel with Hefner's rightful insistence that sex be accepted as natural, good in itself, and healthy. We only wish that he coupled this exuberance for sexual fulfillment with more emphasis on the affectional relationships which make sex ultimately meaningful. For those in the latter half of life he has little to contribute. In fact by stressing the glamour, the excitement, and the value of sex per se, he may be grossly distorting the deep values of sexual fulfillment for those of a later age. Sex as communication of devotion is rarely discussed in *Playboy*, but it is this aspect of coition that means most to those in middle life.

THE ROOTS OF MIDDLE-AGE PROBLEMS

Some of the physiological difficulties that are involved in sex for those in this age group have already been indicated. They were reviewed in relationship to the problem of identity, and that information will not be repeated here. Our task in this chapter is to try to understand the processes of sexual living that bring a couple to middle age with fear or with fulfillment and then to see if we can add such insight that each couple at this stage can have a realistic approach to sex that will be rewarding and fulfilling. Far too many couples have a lack of enthusiasm for each other and for their physical relationships by the time they reach forty. It is this disenchantment in all areas that threatens the second half of life.

When there is no enthusiasm and no life, what remains? Edmund Bergler, who has contributed as much as anyone to our understanding of the middle-aged rebel, sums it up by saying that "a great emptiness remains." Then Bergler goes on to develop for us a consistent frame of reference for understanding the middle-aged man's reaction.[1] When the middle-aged male finds neither psychological nor sexual stimulation at home, says Bergler, he finds a way to evade responsibility by elevating his wife to the position of Enemy

No. 1. Of course she is being tormented by the physical discomforts of menopause and the role readjustments attending child launching so that her behavior is not exactly loving at all times. This causes the man to feel that in his moment of doubt he has been abandoned, and he moves to salvage the situation by looking for a girl friend. Bergler thinks that at this stage two desperations battle. One is an acute tiredness. The other is the man's need to reaffirm his masculinity and his worth by succeeding with another woman.

Bergler does not rest his argument on this description of events. He locates the reaction of the middle-aged person in personality difficulties which stem from early life. The sequence of events is as follows: The baby who is early served and worshiped develops a feeling of omnipotence, "infantile megalomania." When in a few months the child discovers that he is not omnipotent, that many of his wishes are not met with instant fulfillment, he develops anger and later aggression against his mother and father, whom he is taught should be loved. His aggressions against these "people with a halo" are met with *punishment, moral reproach,* and *guilt.* He has to succumb because he is little. As he succumbs, he learns to identify with his parents and their wishes. This helps him feel that he is still in command when he abides by their wishes because he says to himself that he is still doing what he wants to do. Thus he becomes socialized. But, Bergler says, at the same time a second element of the unconscious is developing, which he calls *Daimonion.* This self-destructive factor is the major source of punishment for a person, and comes from the child's "unusable inward-flowing aggression." One part of his conscience identifies with his parents and holds the child's "promise to give the world proof of his power through his future success." The other part constantly contrasts his ideal with real achievements and imposes penance because of the "discrepancy" between what is promised and what is achieved.

These promises a child makes to himself are still operative when he becomes an adult. As no man ever lives up to his dreams he must pay for that failure "in terms of conscious dissatisfaction and guilt." The most important way that an individual counters his dissatisfaction and guilt is by way of what Bergler terms "psychic masochism." The masochist is one who, in childhood, continued to do things which elicited punishment from others. He has continued to express "forbidden wishes," and must therefore find some solution for his pain. He thus learns to "derive pleasure from displeasure." He rationalizes this by the consolation of "being the innocent victim of somebody else's meanness." The process begins with the child's aggression, which changes later to guilt and suffering, and is then resolved by finding pleasure in displeasure.[2]

In middle age the battle between these two elements of the unconscious becomes more heated. *Daimonion,* the self-destructive urge, now taunts the man with his passing years and unhappiness. He may think that by trying to give proof to his youth by a successful affair with a young woman he is improving his situation, but in reality he is only arranging for *one more defeat.* Bergler distinguishes between the conscious rationalization—"Why not fight for youth?"—and the unconscious drive to experience the "inner scourge of pleasurable self-damage." While consciously he is asking for understanding, unconsciously he is seeking out persons who will hurt him.

Bergler offers as evidence for his theory the types of women who respond to middle-aged rovers. His typology comes from a lifetime of clinical practice, but is not otherwise empirically justified. The first of these "understanding" women is called *Miss Injustice Collector.* This girl is herself a masochist or she would not expect great rewards for her investment in a man twice her age. The middle-aged man rarely divorces his wife and marries the girl. She puts herself into a situation she can use later as a source of all the injustices done to her, which she likes to enumerate, and suffering, on which she enjoys ruminating.

The second type is called *Miss Mild Resignation.* She is a "nice, thirtyish, decent girl" who has once been married and quickly divorced. She has whittled down her expectations and asks only for some "warmth and understanding." She does not expect marriage; she expects the man to return to his wife. In fact one such female once said to Bergler, "I'm the Florence Nightingale of half-broken marriages."

The third category of willing, sacrificial females is labeled *Miss Illusion.* She may enter her experiences through naïveté, or she may simply be setting the stage for disillusionment and suffering, but the end result is "self-damage." Her self-deception is only a cover for her unconscious need to be exploited and to suffer.

A fourth type is *Miss Magic Gesture*. Externally she is described as being "kind, motherly, and hyperunderstanding." She "selflessly devotes herself to advancing the happiness of the man." She can make a man feel that for the first time he is loved completely and unselfishly. In fact, says Bergler, she is often so kind that the victim may say to her, "You are an angel." The worse the character of the man the more he appeals to her. But the "angel" finally changes into "an aggressive termagant," and she turns to another "beneficiary" of her gifts.

There are many other types distinguished by Bergler as being susceptible to the tentative invitations of married, middle-aged men. We shall name them quickly, simply to do justice to Bergler's typology. They are *Miss Revenge, Miss Professional Troublemaker, Miss Rescue Fantasy, Miss Gold Digger,* and *Miss Promiscuous*. Bergler's good humor comes out when he remarks about men who get involved with this last type: "It is not rewarding, as some of these elderly men discover who attempt to teach monogamy in an extramarital affair."

The one type of woman who is conspicuously absent from this list is a normal female for, as Bergler says, "If a girl is halfway stable emotionally, she automatically and unconsciously avoids the rebel's hopeless troubles and the problems arising from any relationship with him." This means that the middle-aged rebel can not expect to find any surcease from the sorrow of being misunderstood in his associations with these women.

Bergler concludes this analysis with a famous line that has become the title of another book, *Divorce Won't Help*. He feels that divorce in most cases and certainly in the case of middle-aged masochists is a testimonial to inner conflict in the life of the divorcing person and not always to unsolvable relationship patterns.

Bergler begins and ends his book with a flat assertion that middle-age distress is universal. He does not think this conflict can ever be avoided, and he does not think that the solution is simple. He lists ten possible solutions and rejects nine of them. As the cause of the revolt lies in the unconscious, only a treatment designed to relieve the stresses in the unconscious can be of much assistance. He therefore recommends psychoanalysis as the only way out. There is, however, a natural history to the revolt. The rebel will be defeated. How he handles his defeat is significant for the future. Some kind of adjustment will take place, and it will probably depend on the "stability of the marriage in the period before the second adolescence." Bergler does feel that public awareness of this critical period of the wife's menopausal difficulties and the male's rebellion may help future generations prepare for the storm ahead and handle it more intelligently. This knowledge will help to "cushion the blow." While Bergler shies away from "reasonable advice" he comes close to a positive prescription when he says:

> Relative contentment and middle-age are by no means mutually exclusive. Whining and rebellion, cynicism and over-drinking, lead nowhere. Suffering with dignity, adaptation to reality without blaming it all on the poor wife, making the best of life, short as it is, are difficult but not impossible.[3]

As a final window on Bergler's pessimism we may quote one of his larger generalizations, which sounds much like Camus or Sartre:

> The misery of man is nowhere so clearly and tragically marked as in the transitional years of second adolescence . . .

Most therapists appreciate Bergler's descriptions more than his theory. Little empirical clinical evidence exists to support his contention that psychic masochism is the basic root of either neurosis or the middle-age conflict. He has done a vast service in dramatizing the middle-age revolt as a focus of investigation and attention. His contention that to be aware of possible conflicts and behavior patterns is, in a sense, to be prepared to deal with them is certainly a valid point of view. My own clinical experience with those caught in middle-age conflicts differs from Bergler's in that I have found that (1) the source of difficulty often lies in an inadequate marital relationship as well as in individual psychological history: (2) the presenting problem is often far more complex than Bergler makes it, and combines both the personal and the interpersonal aspects of an individual's history; (3) a great many men, particularly those who have successful business and marital histories, do not exhibit signs of middle-age revolt to any significant degree; and (4) there are other inner sources of the middle-age revolt besides a masochistic reaching for self-punishment. We can look at another study for further insight regarding the sexual problems that lead to extramarital affairs.

Gordon Cumming, as a graduate student at the University of Southern California, studied forty-four males and fifty-four females who were involved in extramarital affairs. They were not limited to the middle-age group, but the results of the study have meaning for middle-age sexual life. One interesting finding is that in twelve of the cases involving males and twenty-two of those involving females, the affair did not involve sexual intercourse. The reasons the married subjects gave for being involved in extramarital affairs were, by rank order, as follows: (1) poor sexual adjustment in marriage; (2) finding the other man or other woman a challenge; (3) being "in love"; (4) having an unaffectionate mate; (5) involvement in a marriage that never was good; (6) enjoyment of the company of the other man or other woman; (7) feeling sympathy for the other man or other woman; (8) getting revenge; (9) no specific reason. Cumming compared the personality profiles of those having affairs, as scored on the Minnesota Multiphasic Personality Inventory, a well-known measure of personality, with norms established for this test in two other studies and concluded that "In light of the results . . . concerning the scores of the subjects they definitely display personality deficiencies as measured by this personality inventory.[4]

The results indicated that (1) the total picture of the subjects as shown on the tests indicated abnormal personalities; (2) the profiles of 40 per cent were rated as abnormal when judged by the norms established by authors of the test; and (3) the marital partners involved in affairs received almost three times as many abnormal scores as a group of Northwestern students used for comparison. Of the group studied forty per cent received abnormally high scores on the Johnson Temperament Analysis scale, which is another type of personality inventory.

Only one third of the males indicated that their motivation for involvement in an affair rested in dissatisfaction with their sexual adjustment in marriage, but almost one fourth of the females rooted their motivation in an inadequate marital relationship which had failed from the beginning. This study indicates that interactional factors either in the marriage or in the relationship with the other man or other woman were responsible for the behavior. This evidence supports our clinical observation that much of middle-age sexual experimentation is compensation for lack of love and companionship in the marriage rather than being due to inner needs to suffer. This does not preclude an awareness of the proclivity individuals with unstable personalities have toward trying to solve their problems by external manipulations rather than by resolving their inner conflicts.

Dorothy and Jim encountered a severe sexual difficulty when Jim was forty-eight and Dorothy was forty-seven. Their case is instructive in illustrating the interrelationship of physiological, psychological, and marital factors in sexual difficulties at this age.

It seemed to me that Dorothy dragged Jim into the office. He responded to my invitation to sit down by turning his chair in such a way that he could not see his wife. He knew what was coming and it came dramatically. Dorothy had hardly hit the chair when she wrenched open her bag and produced the damning testimony—a handkerchief well decorated with purple lipstick, which, it later turned out, Jim had put in the pocket of the car. She threw it on the desk with words she threw at both of us: "Ask him to explain that!"

The husband's head descended into his shoulders, from where he studied the carpet intently. He seemed utterly miserable. I doubted if this were the best moment for his confession, so I slowed up the action by saying; "Wait a minute, Mrs. B——, let me get a little background information before we come to the problems."

Then for ten minutes I elicited some harmless information as to age, length of marriage, children, etc., so that Jim could lift his chin and at least feel that this was not a star chamber for an inquisition. After this I asked Dorothy, not Jim, what she thought the handkerchief indicated. She replied that she didn't think—she knew—Jim had confessed that he was involved with another woman. Once started, she couldn't stop. She recited with great feeling all of her

twenty-five years of service, her loyalty, her long love for Jim now
destroyed by his shameful betrayal. Then, perhaps for emphasis,
she sobbed. It was a typical beginning of such a case; a dramatic
recital of proof, self-justification, angry denunciation, and then sorrow, none of which was designed to ease Jim's guilt or to help us
begin to look objectively at the problem. So, after she had sobbed a
minute, I gently helped her stop by saying that I understood her
feelings, but that we should now get on with the problem, that they
had not really come to me to witness accusations but to see what
could be done. Jim perked up at that and looked at me with some
relief.

When Dorothy could talk again, she was calmer, and said I had
better know the whole story. This was not the only episode of unfaithfulness; another had occurred ten years before. She had wholly
forgiven Jim for that failure, but she didn't know if she could for-
give him for this recent adventure with "that cheap, scheming secretary." The mention of other times led me to ask for some history
of their sexual lives.

They had never achieved a mutually satisfactory sexual relationship. Their history sounded like an outline a professor would give
to a class of marriage counselors in explaining the process of sexual
alienation. Their engagement period had been filled with intermittent attempts at intercourse. But Dorothy had been so afraid of
pregnancy that her vaginal muscles had been taut; the experience
had been painful for Jim and disappointing to her. She had entered
marriage with grave fears that she was "frigid" and, indeed, her
high anxiety during the honeymoon and early adjustment period
precluded any normal sexual response on her part. Jim was exas-
perated and guilty; he blamed himself because he felt that their
premarital experience was the cause of her distress. He also blamed
himself because he could not satisfy her and began to wonder about
his own masculinity. His anxiety produced premature ejaculations,
and this made him hostile to Dorothy. He did not try to bring her
to a point of physical arousal that might cause her to respond, for
he was afraid that if he waited this long she would still fail because
he might have his orgasm even before intromission. So intercourse
became only an exercise to give him relief. He rationalized this

period this way: "I didn't want to stimulate her so that she would later be upset and nervous."

This type of sexual experience had so few rewards that the frequency soon diminished, and was attempted only when Jim was bursting with desire. On some of these attempts he had an orgasm before entry, which made him deeply ashamed and, in his characteristic way, he abruptly turned away from Dorothy instead of continuing to love her and provide her some experience of love and sexual fulfillment, even if not during intercourse. She was, of course, frustrated. They did not manage any discussion of this because Jim felt so belittled that he simply lashed out at her and called her "frigid," while she felt it better simply to endure the problem than to dispute his reproaches.

They did manage to have two children in this period, and Dorothy used the pregnancies to discourage further contact. There is normally a period before birth and after birth when intercourse is proscribed, but Dorothy extended them for many months. As she had never had an orgasm with Jim, and was sensitive to his reproach, she used pregnancy as a means to prevent further humiliation for both of them. After the birth of the second child, she buried herself in the task of raising her children so that whenever Jim came to her she always had to "check" on the children, and was gone so long that his ardor was effectively cooled off. He knew that his attentions were not wanted.

But this meant a great deal more to Jim. This constant rejection confirmed his earlier fear that he had failed as a male. He became obsessed with both his sexual need and his sexual failure, and he lapsed into a depression, which affected his work. His boss called him in, heard the story, laughed at him, and told him, "Get it somewhere else; most men don't do well at home." This rather rough advice made Jim wince, but on reflection he thought he had better try. He tried, but the girl he picked up in a bar was so crude in language and actions that he failed again.

On the eleventh wedding anniversary he confessed to Dorothy what had happened. She was mortified. Her manner of helping in the situation was to begin a series (they lasted for years) of what Jim called "moral lectures." He subsequently gave up the affair, but he had even more difficulty in approaching his wife. He felt that he had to try so that she would not question his faithfulness, but each occasion reinforced his feeling of failure. She was now sexually "dutiful," but never passionate; she "turned him off." Consequently sexual relations were desultory and Dorothy still had not had an orgasm.

By this time the children were in junior high school and gone much of the time; Dorothy knew that she would have to find something to do. She made a few feeble attempts to improve her relations with Jim, but the couple were so alienated that she found no response from him. She began to feel that her husband would never help her be a "complete" female and that he would never be a companion either.

In their fifteenth year together she decided to make a life for herself and enrolled in several courses in night school. She had at this time some vague thoughts that perhaps she could prepare herself for employment and, after the children had graduated from high school, leave Jim. It did not take her long at night school to find a somewhat younger instructor who was very glad to help her achieve womanhood. She justified the experience on the ground that her husband was impotent. It mattered little to the instructor; he was prepared to teach her, regardless of why she wanted to learn. During this period sexual life between Dorothy and Jim diminished to nothing because she could not tolerate having sex with two men. Jim never knew of Dorothy's long affair, which terminated when the instructor left for another school.

In their twentieth year of marriage (Jim was forty-two and Dorothy was forty-one) Jim's doctor made some pointed inquiries about his job satisfaction and his sexual life. During their discussions Jim awakened to the fact that life was passing him by and determined to talk the problem out with Dorothy in an effort to reach some kind of adjustment. He was now achieving good success at work, and the reinforcement which this gave his ego helped him face a problem he had earlier been unable to think about. As Dorothy had been without any sexual life for several years, she welcomed this opportunity to try, and they reached an agreement that for the first time they would try to help each other. They agreed to be patient with each other, and for the next four years they blundered along trying one experiment after another and always failing. They stressed positions, timing, and all sorts of techniques, but what was really needed was some help for Jim's profound anxiety and Dorothy's guilt over her affair. But neither of these could be mentioned; they hurt too much. They tried valiantly to talk about sex during the first two years of their new effort, but after that they expected defeat and only tried by way of satisfying Jim. Dorothy intensified her plans to leave him as soon as she could.

Dorothy was now premenopausal, and her physical and psychological discomfort added to their alienation. She was hemorrhaging heavily during her menstrual periods and becoming somewhat irritated and tense due to endocrine imbalance. Jim was often at a loss to account for his own lack of libido with Dorothy, a result which now was a product of both his anxiety and general aging. They became increasingly tense with each other and finally reached the stage of bitterly projecting their sense of frustration in terms of blaming the other for their sexual and marital failure.

It was during this period that Jim's doctor told him to slow down a bit and his boss had a heart attack. Jim became aware of the need for painful visits to the dentist and of some discomfort when he was swimming. In other words he was in a period of "middle-age panic." While it was not so severe a depression as he had encountered previously, he felt "flat, a failure, demotivated, and just plain unhappy." He was often tired for no good reason. Nor did it help for his doctor to tell him that all men have to adjust to changes in the life cycle. He felt life was almost over. But it was not over for many others, one of whom was a shapely divorcee of thirty who come into Jim's office to replace a girl who had gotten married. This "injustice collector" was attractive, willing, seductive, and sensitive. She easily sensed in Jim's quick interest in her that he had some problems somewhere in his life, and was willing, if possible, to help solve them. Her behavior was always proper, always helpful, and always admiring. It was not long before Jim began to fantasy about her— as she intended him to do—and after awhile people in the office took bets as to how long it would be before the two got together. It was, consequently, almost inevitable that when her car broke down and she needed a ride home from the office, Jim would volunteer and that, once there, they would have some drinks and, after that, would end up in bed. What was surprising was that Jim, having adopted a type of resignation to the whole matter, was able to perform. This of course gave an impetus to his relationship with the girl, who seemed to him to be his salvation. He liked his success, but he hated the deception that went with the escapade. He also began to review his marriage and to contemplate both its failure and its value.

While he gained a somewhat better perspective regarding his relations with Dorothy, he still blamed himself for having deprived her of any sexual success. He worried about the image of masculinity he had furnished for his boy, who was having social difficulties in college. He was really not sure that outside of bed he could be very compatible with his girl friend over a period of time. All this led him to the point of suggesting marital counseling to Dorothy when she found the handkerchief. This particular couple were able to work out their problems and to lay a secure foundation for the second half of life. The other point to be made here is that if they had gone to a counselor before they were married or during their first adjustment difficulties, this history would never have been given. They still might have had some problems at middle age, but not in the degree they faced because of the process of alienation.

We can utilize this case to indicate some specific points about sexual adjustment that may help others to avoid these mistakes. The first point is the intimate and unavoidable relationship of sex in the mid-years to all the things that have gone on before. Healthy sex during this period means healthy love.

SEXUAL ACHIEVEMENT AS PART OF THE MARITAL PROCESS

One day, long past, Elizabeth Barrett Browning slipped into the study where her husband was writing, brushed by him, and in her shyness almost surreptitiously slipped a sheaf of papers into his pocket, and then slipped out of the room. He in some wonder began to read, and in one of the poems he read were these words:

> How do I love thee? Let me count the ways.
> I love thee to the depth and breadth and height
> My soul can reach, when feeling out of sight
> For the ends of Being and ideal Grace.

Sexual intercourse is but one of the ways in which individuals communicate their love to their mates. While coitus reinforces and enriches other aspects of love, it by itself may be impoverished if other strands in the bond of love are frayed and worn. While we concentrated on the specific problems of sexual adjustment of Dorothy and Jim during the middle years, it was with the awareness that adjustment was dependent, too, on the way both the husband and the wife had solved their problems of identity.

We are suggesting that the sexual joy of this or any couple can rarely transcend the general level of satisfaction that a husband and wife have with each other. As we have suggested, many, if not most, marriages are not very spontaneous or rewarding by middle age. The specific way in which this mediocrity of interaction is related to low-level sexual response is devastatingly portrayed in a study by John Cuber and Peggy Harroff, of Ohio State University.[5] They studied upper-middle-class marriages, where all the advantages of prestige and wealth would seem to guarantee a better-than-average relationship. But, as in the case of Blood and Wolfe's middle- and working-class families, these marriages were flat and dull. Cuber and Harroff studied 437 persons of middle age; their subjects were highly educated, economically successful, and personally well adjusted. Those couples in the study who were selected for the married sample had been married for at least ten years, and said that they had never thought of separation or divorce; their ages ranged from thirty-five to fifty-five. The researchers made a unique classification of the kinds of relationships which the couple exhibited. They found the following types:

1. *Conflict-Habituated Relationships*, in which "Incompatibility is pervasive," and "conflict is ever-potential."
2. *Devitalized Relationships*, in which there is neither serious tension nor any "vital meaning." The marriage is "essentially empty."
3. *Passive-Congenial Relationships*, which have "little vitality" but are "passively content."
4. *Vital Relationships*, characterized by "vibrant and excited sharing of some important life experience."

5. *Total Relationships,* in which "all important aspects of life are mutually shared and enthusiastically participated in."[6]

They found most of these upper-middle-class marriages full of "conflict" and "apathy"; few were really satisfying. The researchers made the point again and again that the marriages had no vitality, that they were "passive" and "dull."

We are particularly interested in Cuber and Harroff's report on the result this "passivity" had on the sexual lives of the couples. Some wives described their sexual lives as "legal prostitution, not much better than masturbation." And the husbands, grown tired of their mates, thought of them as "legal, inexpensive, clean mechanisms for physical gratification." That this was not a measure of their latent sexual capacity was shown when some of the men and women who were thought by their mates to be either "unaffectionate" or "frigid" reported that they were most responsive in love affairs outside the marriage. It is this lack of affection that interests us particularly.

I would like to recall two previous points. The first and most significant one is that as children leave the immediate family, there is no one else left to give affection to the wife other than the husband and vice versa. The second point is that, as Blood and Wolfe said, the husband's expression of love and affection *decreased* steadily with the years. Thus all our research comes together at this critical issue of lack of adequate sexual expression. For when there is no intimacy, no demonstrations of affection, and little tenderness, sex is indeed meaningless, and tends to become devitalized. It is understandable that many middle-aged persons who have allowed their total marriage to become passive would likewise find their sexual mate uninspired.

SEXUAL ACHIEVEMENT AND CREATIVE DEMONSTRATION OF AFFECTION

But even where there is warmth and affection, the marriage can be full of ennui. When a husband and wife reach forty-five, they have been married, perhaps, twenty-five years, and they are used to each other. There is one constant refrain that middle-aged women use in describing their sexual lives. A recent client said:

> Certainly I get headaches or a tired back to avoid sex with my husband. That is programmed. He never calls me. He spends the dinner hour ten miles away and never talks to me. After dinner there is the paper and the idiot box. But suddenly he becomes aware of me when we get in bed. Then I can predict every word, every gesture until I think I'll go mad. If he changed that routine I'd be so surprised I probably would have a stroke or laugh or something. Sex isn't an adventure . . . it hasn't been for twenty years . . . it's like I said, a routine. Sure I get headaches . . . I also get bored.

Although Elizabeth Barrett Browning was talking about a much broader concept when she said, "How do I love thee? Let me count the ways," her delight in the variety and creativity of ways of showing her affection for her husband could be applied to making love. Sexual response depends on stimulus, but as Isadore Rubin well emphasizes, "The same stimulus, repeated too often, gradually loses its effect." Then comes boredom and fatigue. As couples become adjusted, they all too often become routinized, and there is not more novelty or excitement in their lovemaking than in dressing. As a couple ages, both the man and the woman require new experiences.

New experiences in the sexual realm are not just physical. However, if a couple have never used more than one position for twenty-five years or varied their repertoire of love-play gestures, there is no *play* left in their approaches. It is a truism now to say that any precoital type of stimulation is both moral and valuable, provided that it is not disgusting to either partner. Nevertheless, the problem is not so much the morality of new sexual approaches as it is to habit. Habit is the master of the unimaginative. And a habit becomes so automatic that it commands little attention. Thus habit in sexual activities cannot produce anything but lack of passion and response. Maxine Davis, author of *The Sexual Responsibility of Woman*, thinks that the male is in need of special stimulation so that "From middle age on, a wife had better take steps to jolt her husband out of his rut."[7] The experiences of the people I see in my clinic are somewhat different.

The transition from the old passive female role to that of a creative equal partner is only half accomplished in society and half accomplished in the sexual sphere. Dorothy could have helped Jim more than she did. It is true that many men are delighted when, sitting in their living room, their wives suddenly appear behind their chair, kiss them behind the ear, and gently ease toward the bedroom. It is also true that some men are offended by sexual initiative on the part of women. They still feel that that is the male prerogative, and a sexually aggressive partner would find nothing but rejection from them. There is no reason why the female should not have as much right as the male to indicate sexual need or desire. But if a woman has not felt free to initiate coital relations until she is forty-five, it is difficult for her to suddenly switch and become more active than she was during her early marriage. Maxine Davis may be right, but her prescription does not fit all male expectations.

What seems more fitting is that all through marriage both the male and female should strive in their precoital and coital activity to please the other. This ought to be the subject of honest discussion and much experimentation. If this is the case, when middle age comes, the couple's progress in sexual ingenuity and creativity will be such that no special shifts in their approach will be necessary. Nevertheless, it is true, as Davis says, that "it is never too late or too soon to open new doors to adventure and romance."

SEXUAL ACHIEVEMENT AND FREQUENCY

There are physiological concomitants to the passive and intermittent sexual attempts of many middle-aged couples. Sexual organs, like many others of the body, respond to use and atrophy with disuse. If a couple are sexually bored with each other and consequently have a parsimonious sexual life, they will pay a price in the lack of full facility for intercourse. William H. Masters and Virginia E. Johnson, as the result of studying 152 older women, say:

Frequently women from five to 10 years postmenses who experience infrequent coition (once a month or less) and who do not masturbate with regularity have difficulty in accommodating the penis during their rare exposures to coition. It is also true that many younger women deprived of coital opportunity for long periods of time may have to contend with a slowed rate of vaginal lubrication and restricted vaginal-barrel expansion during a first return to coital connection.[8]

They hold that the same factor of continued interest and participation in sexual activity is important in maintaining the sexual vigor of the male:

> The most important factor in the maintenance of effective sexuality for the aging male is consistency of active sexual expression. When the male is stimulated to high sexual output during his formative years and a similar tenor of activity is established for the 30–40 year age range, his middle-aged and involutional years usually are marked by constantly recurring physiologic evidence of maintained sexuality.[9]

In this sense it is true that to him that hath shall be given, and to him that tries there is the reward. But if ennui and devitalization destroy sexual response, the physiologic result is a growing inability to respond. This is not to say that a fifty-year-old man ought to expect the same vigor that he had at twenty. There is a gradual change with the years, and this must be expected. If it is resisted with fear, the middle-age crisis becomes a middle-age panic, and nothing but trouble follows.

The sexual union in the late forties and fifties probably will not be marked with as much passion as it was right after the honeymoon but it has new depths of meaning. All the experiences of the past are now included in the devotion of one to the other. There is less passion, but more love. Emily H. Mudd, former director of *Marriage Council* in Philadelphia, says:

> Sex in the middle and later years has a unique meaning for each couple. Hopefully, maturity has brought with it release from the conflicts of youth and from the externally imposed conformity of young adulthood. Sexuality can then become the intimate expression of love and chosen union between two beings. As the benefits of high levels of health, and increased leisure for men as well as women, are extended, we might expect sex to become an increasingly meaningful experience in the middle years. Generativity is not limited to the creation of a life; it is the substance of living.[10]

It is of course this sense of generativity in middle-aged persons that is so often lacking. It is certainly absent from all those marriages where the characteristic emotion is boredom. Joseph Trainer not only notes the critical importance of this factor in his chapter on "The Special Malady—Tired Wives and Husbands," but he also has some suggestions regarding the possibility of replacing "weary plodding" with enthusiasm:

> One of the most common disappointments people express in marriage (and it is usually the wife who expresses it) is the lack of expected companionship. In essence this problem is the failure to share enthusiasms. The partners become unwilling, uncomfortable roommates, sharing a space without sharing each other. . . . Each partner must bring enthusiasm to the cultivation of the other. Life is not status and marriage is more than legalized sex. We live in so many facets and modes, and in each possible way we need to cultivate the other. And we need to receive the enthusiasm of the other. . . . The husbands and wives who cannot focus on anything but the chore and impending crisis are liabilities to themselves and their households. If they are totally unable to get a charge out of the small triumphs of the day, they will have no exuberance to communicate to each other. Into each life some enthusiasm must fall; else there is no life.[11]

SEXUAL ACHIEVEMENT AND ENDOCRINE BALANCE

If we can summarize what we have said in the previous chapter about male and female endocrine balance it would be to simply reiterate that great strides are being taken to assure women of such continuous supplies of estrogen that they will not find physical difficulties during middle age troublesome. But this contribution to health also assures the contemporary female of defenses against the atrophy of vaginal cells and loss of libido so that she need suffer no organ deficiencies to militate against her full sexual response during these years. Some gynecologists report that the new freedom from fear of pregnancy increases sexual desire. The woman has a new sense of abandon in her sexual experience. Furthermore, the children are gone so that for perhaps the first time in twenty years there is real privacy at home. If minor problems, such as the loss of lubrication fluids, cause irritation there are now estrogenic suppositories which take care of such local problems as well as stimulating the vaginal cells. This was one problem that was successfully solved for Dorothy.

While these advantages are all possible for modern women, many are not using them. Some women have heard widely publicized stories about the negative effects of hormone treatment, which cause them to be afraid. In such a case the woman ought to consult her gynecologist immediately and follow his advice. While we are relatively sure, due to a study of the literature, that these cautions are exaggerated, the proper recommendation in medical matters is to follow medical advice. A marriage counselor investigates problems, but then refers the client to his or her doctor for final recommendations.

The male does not have the same problem, and the same recommendations do not apply to him. His potency can last far into old age, provided that he maintains a sensible health regime, is not psychologically disturbed, and does not abandon his sexual practices. Our word for him is simply to trust his physical nature and not be disturbed by a few failures, which are natural with aging.

SEXUAL ADJUSTMENT AND COMMUNICATION

However, timing is an essential point in sexual adjustment after forty. Neither the man nor the woman has the reserves of energy which he or she possessed at twenty. Both may be more involved in economic or community enterprises that are psychologically taxing than they were at a younger age. The man is at the height of his economic achievements, and must necessarily invest a good deal of energy at the very time his reserves are diminishing. This means that even though, intellectually, he would like to be sexually active, his pace is naturally slowing down. Kinsey found that there is a normal curve of attrition in sexual life for both men and women. If the couple realize this, and do not mind a somewhat greater interval between the occasions of sexual love, they will find greater response and enjoyment of their efforts. It seems, however, that a great many individuals in our society sacrifice sexual life for status struggles. During the middle years it is a good thing to be fully aware of the costs of our investments. Some individuals choose to put the brake on work so that they may enjoy recreation, social life, and sexual activities to a greater degree. They also live longer.

All these adjustments can be made without friction and with growing appreciation of the mate if there is freedom of communication by this age. But freedom of communication is a scarce commodity in middle age. Jessie Bernard, distinguished family sociologist, concluded, after reviewing research literature and reports on husband-

wife relationships, that "conversation, 'just plain talk' between husband and wife never happens ... people become habituated to one
another, but this is a far cry from companionship."[12]

Jim and Dorothy failed completely in the sporadic efforts they
made during their marriage to listen to each other and to each other's
needs. Had they been able to shed their defensiveness and earnestly
try to understand the ego needs of the other, they would have had
a better chance of improving their behavior in bed. If the couple
cannot talk about sex and about the gestures that are pleasing and
needed during the middle age, they probably should seek out a
therapist to help them release their hostilities or inhibitions so that
they can move toward better adjustment.

SUMMARY

Most couples find that their sexual adjustment during middle age
is a product of the history of their total relationship during their
marriage. The middle-age crisis comes because past devotion or
communication is inadequate to give foundation for meeting the
new problems of this period. If there is openness between husband
and wife so that fears and needs can be openly shared, answers can
be worked out. Medical science has provided new help to ease the
transition, to make intercourse much more rewarding during this
period. If there are significant physical or relationship problems,
they could be referred to a physician or a marriage counselor. There
can be zest and enthusiasm in this as well as in all other areas if
aging is accepted as normal and rewarding. Our task in the next
chapter is to try to discover how zest and enthusiasm can be re-
tained in social, family, and recreational aspects of living.

6

Making
the Most of the
Mid-Years

Is it possible to avoid the disenchantment with marriage and with life that seems to characterize so many persons in our society? I think it is, provided that old habits and expectations are abandoned in favor of new life patterns and new attitudes. Past sources of satisfaction in the bearing and rearing of children are no longer available to fathers and mothers in their mid-forties or their mid-fifties. The whole focus of the earlier twenty years of marriage must change. It is this necessity to match changing family size and function with new activities and interests that challenges us in this chapter. As I have explained previously, such a radical shift in situation has never before occurred in history so that few models are available to copy and it is necessary to develop initiative and enterprise in exploring new pathways to satisfaction. The challenge to make the last half of marriage as significant as the first half is easier to identify than to meet. In this chapter we explore ways of leaving the past and exploring the present and future. Life has to be different in these years, but it does not have to be inferior to years past.

DIMENSIONS OF A SATISFYING LIFE

Several authors have explored ways of achieving zest and enthusiasm during the latter half of life. Robert J. Havighurst has devoted much of a productive life to determining dimensions that would assure life satisfaction to middle-aged and older persons. He likes to think of these years as the "prime of life," and his recommendations come out of long research into the problems of aging.[1] Havighurst emphasizes the necessity of changing one's posture and developing a new kind of wisdom which is consonant with role changes and health levels during middle age.

The first dimension, suggests Havighurst, is *valuing wisdom versus valuing physical powers*. The loss of the urgency of sexual drive, the increase of general fatigue, and the growing awareness of some aches and pains combine to convince the middle-aged person that he is no longer eighteen years old. Havighurst feels that it is important to accept these declines in libido and energy levels and to move from absorption with muscle satisfactions to mental concerns.

Two dangers need to be highlighted here. Some middle-aged men and women focus so exclusively on symptoms of aging that they become almost hypochondriacal. Others go through the sexual rebellion studied in the last chapter in an effort to disprove to themselves the fact that they are, in reality, growing older. Both of these coping mechanisms are disastrous. It has already been suggested that sexual life can be just as satisfying as ever if one accepts a frequency of sexual contact that is harmonious with energy levels. It is also possible to enjoy such activities as athletics, hiking, and games if participation is moderate and, again, in keeping with one's age limitations. When a sixty-year-old man insists on swimming for miles in the ocean every day of the year, he is not promoting his health or demonstrating good mental health. I have known several men who used this dramatic means to deny their gray hair and shortness of breath.

Havighurst suggests that middle age is the period in which to substitute thinking and the wisdom that comes from maturity for physical satisfactions. Indeed he thinks that one can accomplish a great deal more during this period than earlier because mental effort concentrates on "things that are really important." What is being suggested here modifies Havighurst's point of view somewhat because he puts *wisdom* and *physical powers* in opposition. Is it not possible to retain much of the satisfaction that comes from physical powers, but done in moderation, while at the same time increasing the amount of reward found in mental explorations? It is not certain that the heart specialists would agree to Havighurst's proposition that "the principal means of coping with life shifts from the use of physical energy to the use of wisdom." It is rather a new *balance* between the two that is to be maintained for maximum health and satisfaction. It is true that if other rewards are not gradually substituted for the "decrease in physical vigor and attractiveness" there will be "feelings of failure and inadequacy," but the suggestion ought to be rephrased as follows: an increasing valuing of wisdom along with a realistic valuing of physical powers. Despite these modifications, Havighurst's stress on accepting aging as natural and on the development of new avenues of satisfaction is basic.

The second dimension of success in middle age is *emotional expansion versus emotional constriction*. Havighurst mentions the departure of children and the death of parents, friends, and relatives as events which inevitably will constrict the number of persons available to love and enjoy. This can mean an "impoverishment of emotional life." One must consider, too, the high mobility of American life, which frustrates lifelong friendships and makes us, in a sense, emotional nomads. Two factors are operating here. One is the process of the family cycle. Husbands and wives at middle age reach the stage where their parents die and their children leave. The other factor is industrialization, which puts a premium on moving, so that few of us live near those with whom we were brought up—whether we are speaking of our brothers or sisters or the boys and girls across the street. There are two alternatives: one may suffer emotional deprivation or one may embark on a period of enriching emotional satisfactions by finding new friends and new ways of expressing maternal and paternal feelings in society. There is little reward in the first because individuals who drift into emotional isolation begin too early to live in the past and to feel that life is over. One of the possible compensations for the departure of children has already been suggested, and that is renewal of intimacy with the mate. Another compensation is reaching out to other individuals who, because they are in the same age span, are likewise deprived and lonely. A third way of keeping emotionally alive is to begin to share in the great redemptive work of society in all its efforts to make life more comfortable and productive for those who are handicapped in some way. Furthermore, both the husband and wife now have the time and financial resources to broaden their contacts and their investment in others.

The third dimension for satisfaction in middle age suggested by Havighurst is *mental flexibility versus mental rigidity.* He says that by middle age a relatively fixed set of attitudes on all matters is developed which automatically determines reactions to life. This means that one may be mentally rigid. On the other hand James Birren, also studying at the University of Chicago, came to the conclusion that one of the real assets of middle age is the presence of tested ways of meeting problems which have been validated through the years. Birren says that when one has to make a decision during these years, the experience of the first half of life prepares him with a background of successful ways that make life more efficient.[2] This may be part of the wisdom which Havighurst praised.

The dilemma raised by both Havighurst's analysis of growing rigidity and Birren's tested ways of problem solving is the changing world. Old methods do not always fit anymore, even if they worked well previously. Certainly the computer and the programmed production line have troubled many older workers who were brought up with the adding machine or a hammer in their hands. The cities in which most of us live are also changing. Pollution, transportation, education, race relations, housing, and a dozen more difficult problems are not going to be solved by old attitudes, for those attitudes produced the problems. If the middle-aged man is to have any relevance to the solution of the vexing difficulties facing urban society, he must discard much that he took for granted all his life and indeed develop mental flexibility. Mental rigidity really means mental inactivity. To be rigid is to be fixed; any mental exertion is precluded. Thus in a sense mental rigidity is already intellectual death. To sacrifice the keen instrument of the mind to the woeful comfort of disuse is certainly to give up one of the most exciting ventures of middle age. More will be said about this later in this chapter.

The fourth dimension suggested by Havighurst is *the expansion of interest beyond the work role.* In a sense this is the first period of life in which it is economically feasible to face away from the grind-stone. When two children are in college one cannot ease off. But with the independence of children and the contraction of financial obligations there is a possibility for some relaxation from work. This does not suggest that one does not continue to find a major satis-faction in life from his vocation. If the job fits him, it is a way in which he establishes his sense of making a worthwhile contribution to society, in which he finds confidence in his own value as an indi-vidual, and in which he constantly sharpens his mental tools. Many women find achievement in jobs to be a worthwhile substitute for child rearing. We are not suggesting giving up work at this period, but rather adding a number of new avenues to self-actualization to the satisfactions work brings. Havighurst suggests "the development of leisure activities or putting more investment into clubs, church, civic life, homemaking, friendships or some other form of creative expression." And this achievement of a broader base for satisfaction is essential not only for middle-age adjustment but also as prepara-tion for retirement.

The last of Havighurst's recommendations is that there must be *body transcendence versus body preoccupation.* Aware of the decline in physical vigor at middle age, Havighurst says that this is a crip-pling blow to most people. The reasons he thinks this is so important is that most people "have invested a great deal of emotional capital in their physical appearance and well-being." An equally important reason is the reinforcement of concern for youthfulness in our society. The approved female is not the thirty-eight-year-old mother of three children, but the nineteen-year-old unmarried adolescent. The male that all men admire is the strong-muscled athlete of the teens and early twenties. It is not so much physical vigor that we admire as the "youthful body beautiful." When we see evidence that that body is aging, we panic. And if we do panic, we become preoccupied with the body. This may happen to an even greater degree to those who discover they are somewhat limited by some chronic condition. Havighurst approves giving enough attention to diet, exercise, and dress to feel as well as possible, but he cautions against allowing normal physical aging to be viewed in such a way that depression or panic destroys the possibility of new definitions of happiness and comfort. There are now new opportunities for "satisfying human relationships and creative mental activities which will survive the physical decline of the body."

Havighurst concludes his discussion with these words:

> Just before the prime of life, when a man or woman is working most efficiently and meeting the demands of life most successfully, it is true in a paradoxical way that he is least free. . . . He has little freedom. . . . People can be happy and free and young in spirit in their middle-age and for a long time afterward if they do some personal stock-taking and planning for this period in their lives.[3]

THE FIVE C's OF GROWTH IN THE MIDDLE YEARS

John Walker Powell (a noted adult educator who helped Clark Tibbitts and Wilma Donahue prepare *Aging in Today's Society,* in which Havighurst's discussion of life dimensions appears) says that in middle age there is both time and need for asking questions. He goes on to isolate what he calls "the three C's," which form the basis for growth through the middle-age period: *Curiosity, Creativeness,* and *Comprehension.*[4] We will add two more C's to the list and talk at length about the importance of *Compassion* and *Commitment.*

Curiosity

The degree of curiosity a person has is the measure of the range of his interests. Those who are insatiably curious ask the questions Powell indicates are necessary for adjustment in the second half of life. Curiosity is directed imagination. The curious person wonders why things are as they are, how they got to be that way, and if they can change. The curious mind is the penetrating kind in opposition to the complaining type. When any problem, be it that of aging or any other, confronts any individual, he has the alternatives of ignoring it, grappling with it constructively, or complaining about it. Denial of change rarely works, but there are many middle-aged men and women who *deny* their age. They act as though they were still adolescents. Their friends are often disturbed by this incongruous behavior and tell them to "act their age." We often describe the man who must resort to this type of behavior as the "old fool." Another form of denial behavior is the constant obliteration of awareness by alcohol or by drugs so that reality does not have to be faced. This answer also takes its toll.

The alternative of complaining about or fighting against change does not alter the situation either. Anger, frustration, and complaining never change anything, but instead result in the alienation of others. All of us know dozens of persons who have given up trying to adapt and whose inner adjustment is the expression of irritation. Even worse is the uneasy suspension of some persons in anxiety. Anxiety is a kind of indefinite worry about some ill-defined fear, a gloomy foreboding of possible disaster hovering in the wings of life. Many individuals at fifty give up because they feel that death is around the corner. They retire from everything. I have known three men who have said verbally and by their behavior: "I am fifty; life is over. I give up!" Such a person succumbs to that middle-age syndrome which technically is known as *hypochondriasis*—a morbid and exaggerated preoccupation with illness. He takes his pulse, concentrates on minor pains, causes adrenalin to shoot through his body, and eventually completely cripples his effectiveness.

Such a person drives family, friends, and neighbors out of their minds. Worry as a mental mechanism means negative imagining. People who worry are sometimes quite inventive about situations. They magnify every small slight into something monumental. The man with indigestion staggers to the doctor, certain that he is going to die from a heart attack. The anxious individual differs from the curious in that his fear precludes any *balanced appraisal;* all is threatening and all is negative. He is involved with the problem, but his mood precludes anything but a circular descent into a narrow pit of fear. This is not what Socrates meant when he urged us to examine our lives. The process of worry, anger, and complaint is never examination; the individual has made the judgment before he began his hour of gloomy rumination. The pivotal point is his lack of freedom to examine.

Curiosity depends on freedom from anxious concern. It has many of the attributes of the scientific method. To be really curious is to cast away previous answers and be open to novel insights. By now it is clear that nothing less than innovative solutions will give us the necessary answers, for the answers we found in the child-rearing time of life were for other questions. The need to concentrate on those problems is over. So are the rewards. To deny that fact does not change it. Nor can one dissolve it in alcohol. Complaining does not ease the problem. There is now new freedom from work and more time to ask new questions and discover new answers. Curiosity about new dimensions for one's personal life will help, but curiosity about life itself will help more. An honest acceptance of the situation at mid-life is important, but even more rewarding is the development of ways to enlarge life's horizons.

Which horizons can be enlarged? It is too simple to say all of them, but that is the correct answer. A great many writers have stressed one or another avenues to fulfillment. Some suggest a new interest in arts, others suggest travel, still others want to combine travel with art, and others think that this is the time for new studies in politics and world affairs. One would not limit the possibilities. But whatever avenues for growth are chosen ought to represent genuine interests that can be developed for the rest of a lifetime and not to be performed in a sporadic, dilettante manner. One is building now for all of the second half of life, and this is a norm to bear in mind when choosing interests. The new interests also ought to represent something husband and wife can do together, or at least in complementary ways.

Havighurst, Powell, and Grattan all stress the fact that middle-aged persons have a "special affinity for the reflective disciplines," and they catalog some of the good reading that will sharpen the wits and "clarify one's personal insights." No doubt a valuable investment of the increment of new leisure that comes with reduced family responsibilities is in rereading books that have stimulated in the past or in reading new books that one did not get to because of time pressures. A Great Books group has scope and offers group discussion. Literature does cast a spotlight on life. A great poem, a penetrating play, a novel that illuminates the great issues of life help us to experience life more deeply.

Each year I read Romain Rolland, Maxwell Anderson, Henry Adams, some parts of the Bible, Keats, St. Francis of Assisi, Kahlil Gibran, and some memorable flights of Arthur Conan Doyle's imagination in his mysteries. But these are my diet, and may mean little to another person. The critical thing is to read both the old and the new. John R. R. Tolkien is as exhilarating as Homer; to meet his "little people" in *The Hobbit*[5] is as full of fantasy and delight as to wage again the Trojan War with Achilles.

There are other areas in which a middle-aged man or woman needs to read, just to catch up with what was happening intellectually while each was bent toward the tasks of child raising and occupational achievement. Human knowledge was not arrested during those years; it developed with grand strides, and many middle-aged persons would not recognize either the terms or the concepts in fields in which they were once at home. Many of the physical and the social sciences have changed in exciting ways. The world does not have the same look as it did twenty-five years ago; nor does medicine, dentistry, or psychiatry.

Certainly some aspects of psychological and sociological research are particularly relevant to the middle-aged person. The whole concept of the family life cycle, reviewed in Chapter 2, gives a rewarding perspective from which to view middle age. One could not invest time more wisely than in reading Evelyn Duvall's 1957 book on *Family Development*[6] or any one of a number of Havighurst's studies in the same field. My own book *Education for Marriage*[7] spells out in detail the changes in the American family which are background for understanding the poignancy of the adjustments of the middle years. The book from which we have been quoting in this chapter, *Aging in Today's Society*, edited by Clark Tibbitts and Wilma Donahue, gathers together much of the best thoughts of the sociologists and educators who have seen the challenge of middle age. Sociology has developed both conceptual systems and scientific ways of evaluation which concentrate on smaller units of the social process and which have more accuracy than the grand theorists of the past. A whole new specialization is developing in the field of aging called *gerontology* which is contributing more and more insight to both middle-aged and older persons. Because sociologists are dealing precisely with the family development cycle and with changes that inevitably affect every person in the mid-years, it has much insight to offer those who are curious enough to want to cushion their transition into this period with solid thought from research.

Psychology, too, has much to offer. One of the great revolutions that is taking place in American thought is the reformation of psychological thinking; it is moving away from the pessimistic, deterministic position of Freud to a much broader statement of personality. The new emphasis is on self-actualization and personality growth during all periods of life. One of the most stimulating studies reported is that of Erik Erikson in his book, *Childhood and Society*,[8] which interprets the life cycle in psychological terms, seeing each age of man as a growth period in which something new and broader is added to the individual's development. Perhaps we have passed by the profound insights of such a book as *Toward a Psychology of Being*[9] by Abraham H. Maslow, a psychologist, in which he stresses the normal and the whole person. While this book is solidly based on analysis of contemporary psychology, it is not so difficult that the average person could not grasp it. If he worked through it, his feeling about his middle-age problems might change.

Great strides are being taken in the field of physiology to understand sexual response and the relationship of the libido to aging processes. Two eminent scientists, William H. Masters and Virginia E. Johnson, have written about their research in a controversial book called *Human Sexual Response*.[10] Strangely, most of the criticism of that book is directed at their methods of research and not at the careful conclusions they present. Few reviewers have mentioned the last section of their study called "Geriatric Sexual Response," which offers as valuable a commentary on sex in the middle and later years as one can find anywhere. A few medical terms are used in the book, but this section (which is of particular relevance to middle-aged persons) is singularly lucid and free of technical language. This book likewise contributes a positive point of view which should help many men and women approach their mid-years with confidence and, perhaps, gratitude. A good deal of emphasis is laid here because in a sense most of us were brought up in the shadow of either religious or psychological assumptions that darkened hopes and stressed the abnormal.

If it seems that I am recommending a reading course to cure the difficult dilemmas of middle age, I would hastily correct that impression. These illustrations of change in the sciences are presented here for two purposes: to illustrate the kinds of insight that are available for understanding ourselves, and to introduce some of the changes of goals and methods in social science that may have eluded most of us while we were busy with economic and other matters. Other intellectual fields have changed, too, and have as much to offer in understanding the broader areas of social and political change.

One insistent theme that has been sounded in our defense of democracy as a way of life has been that there is a need for an educated populace. Certainly the multiplication of one person's stupidity by others equally dense does not build the great society. It is only when an informed and critically minded citizen sharpens his wisdom by dialogue with his neighbor that democracy may be seen as more effective than, let us say, an "enlightened monarchy." To have an educated public does not mean that each person must have gone through high school or college. It means rather that each has wrestled positively with such emergent problems as the growing concentration of minority groups in the centers of our cities, the growing conflict between those have-nots and the haves in the suburbs, the concentrations of both gases and frustrations resulting from choked freeways, the steady despoilation of streams, mountains, and forests by the constant growth of population, the utter rejection of an ugly and seemingly callous world by a surprising number of adolescents, the manufacture and stockpiling of such bombs that in this hour it is possible for a false message to turn the earth into a furnace.

Along with such achievements as greater longevity, better health, and the reduction of poverty have appeared the new lethal horses of the apocalypse. Denial or complaints about those monumental problems will not make them go away. Who can contribute to their solution? It seems almost sure that the solution must come from the wisdom of middle-aged men and women who, at their stage of life, have the wisdom and the time to be deeply involved in their reading, in their thinking, and in their dialogues with these specters of destruction. It is heartening that some adolescents are involved actively in the important issues of the day. Adults ought to welcome such involvement as a sign of what the youngsters will be able to do tomorrow, when experience has lengthened their perspective and tempered their passion. But no one really expects them to work out final solutions. Nor have we been uniformly pleased with the relegation of the solution of these problems to the politicians.

Creativeness and Comprehension

When we discuss solutions we are already talking about *creativity*. To be creative means to discover new ways of putting things together whether they be symbols, words, ideas, colors, sounds, people, or buildings. It is the capacity to play new roles and to give novel responses, to look freshly at old things and to discover the relevance of old truths for new situations. This, too, depends on being free enough from anxiety and habit to be able to venture into the unknown and work there. Curiosity may lead us into strange new valleys of experience, but creativeness is the difference between passivity and contribution. It is not enough for the middle-aged citizen to visit the Negro ghetto or to smell the smog and become aware of their dangers. To be a creative citizen, he must learn something about the reasons for the ghetto and pollution so that his voice and his vote make a difference for the black citizen and prevent bad lungs tomorrow. He may have to read many books, listen to many experts, and learn new fields in order to be relevant, but relevant he must be. We are reminded here of the sad comment of the city planner who, after his sabbatical, stated that "capacity is wasted on the middle-aged." Can the middle-aged person, who, in a sense abandoned his intellectual career when he graduated from college, pick it up again twenty years later? One of the notable conclusions of the various studies carried on during the last fifteen years at the Human Development Center at the University of Chicago is that intelligence and comprehension have no age limits. The middle-aged person has lost little of his mental agility. He can comprehend the situation. Whether he is motivated to share creatively is a far more critical issue.

One may be permitted to differ a little from Havighurst and

Powell in their insistence that the whole emphasis be put on the *reflective* disciplines. I have already indicated that I think middle-aged persons are critically needed as activists, albeit informed activists, in the political arena. But there are a great many ways in which life at mid-term may expand its horizons.

Two couples illustrate some other and growing ways of turning from a complete absorption in work and children to new horizons. One couple, Dorothy and Henry, are in their late forties; he is a lawyer and she a housewife. As Dorothy and Henry came home from the wedding reception of their last child, they stopped at their front door and Dorothy broke into sobs: "I don't think I'll ever enjoy this house again without the kids' laughter. It'll be like a tomb."

Henry did some quick thinking and suggested that they take a drive together. They went back to the car, and Henry drove to a high point on a nearby mountain where they had often parked years before during their courtship. They snuggled close to each other and in that hour found some answers to what they both had dreaded as a terminal point to the significance of their lives. But this was only the beginning.

That summer Henry planned a long vacation. Since he knew that Dorothy had enjoyed taking pictures of her children, he bought her a new camera for the trip. They went into the woods of the Northwest, where they pursued the deer and antelope with their camera. One day Henry came upon Dorothy rather idly sketching a hillside scene on her stationery. The next day he brought back a sketch pad and some pastel pencils from his grocery shopping. Dorothy was delighted. As they passed through northern Idaho on their way home they overheard a husband and wife in the next restaurant booth discussing the garnets they had found that day. Henry introduced himself and asked questions. The next day they set off to Garnet Gulch and, having struggled over the hill, brought back ten pounds of perfect specimens. On the rest of their trip home they stopped at every rock shop to learn about the gems and minerals of that locality. They did not have time to hunt for them, but they stored up maps and sketches.

Since then Dorothy and Henry have extended their vacations

each year. Now they pack painting gear, photographic equipment, rock hammers, fishing poles, bird and flower books along with boots and tent. During the winter they make short trips to nearby mineralogical areas or to the ocean to hunt for good pictures or beach agates. Their evenings are spent developing pictures, painting, designing jewelry to display their agate cabochons or their faceted gems. Of course their married children complain occasionally that Mother and Dad seem too busy to baby-sit when they would like to have the weekend off, but they are really overjoyed at their parents' new horizons of interest and fulfillment.

Dorothy will never win a first-class prize in painting. Her photographs grow better through the years, but she has never thought to open a salon of photography. Henry can make a fly light within a few feet of a log, but he also loses a great many of them when he hits the log instead of the deep dark pool beside it. Yet he generally has enough good casts to bring fresh fish back to the tent for dinner, and Dorothy has learned enough about color photography to capture the magic of a rainbow trout sizzling in a big black frying pan. They have learned a good deal about geology, so that they can identify strata and rocks and likely permantites for exploration. They have learned much about botany, and their books on flower species and bird life are well worn. Through their interest in gems they came to study fossils, and one cabinet in their home is devoted to fossilized fish, leaves, and other specimens they have dug up in their journeys. Because they came to be more and more appreciative of nature they joined several of the leading conservation groups that work for the preservation of wildlife and mountains and forests. There they found new friends and new avenues for social expression. Because Henry was a lawyer his skills were utilized in the struggle for conservation. You may meet them sometime on a mountain pass or in the desert. Although it is now twenty years later and they are nearing seventy, their interests are as fresh and their minds as alert as that night when Henry suggested they take a new look at their city.

Henry and Dorothy sometimes visit Mort and Audrey, a couple who would not dream of pitching a tent. When Henry and Dorothy were "lifting up their eyes unto the hills," Audrey and Mort found their way in a much less arduous manner. Mort was a cameraman for a studio, and he had had a difficult time financially in educating his four bright children. Audrey had so concentrated on the children that their leaving had left her without a role. She was well on the road to becoming a "complaining witch" when Mort decided something had to be done. Remembering that Audrey had majored in art history, he proposed that they save their money just as stringently as before and go to Europe to visit the Louvre, the Salt Mine Exhibit, the cathedrals. Audrey objected; she said she'd had enough of poverty, and wanted to spend a little money. But Mort persisted and eventually they found their way to Normandy. There all of Audrey's earlier interests in art were rekindled. She spent hours at Chartres and Notre Dame and at the Louvre. She came home determined to renew her interest in art history. Today she is a respected lecturer in the field. Like the interests Henry and Dorothy found, art history opened up for Audrey and Mort new fields of interest, such as the art film, new organizational memberships, new friendships, and new avenues of service. Both Audrey and Mort have served many years on the boards of influential galleries and art schools. When Mort reached fifty-seven he retired so that he could spend some years producing the type of creative film he had always wanted to do. Obviously Audrey is not a "complaining witch" any more. She is an exciting companion who knows a great deal and who shares a great deal in many significant ways.

There is a reason for telling the stories of these two couples. I could have told a hundred others of individuals who had begun to shrivel up but have grown instead, but these vignettes were chosen because they are about people who are not geniuses. They are really quiet ordinary as far as talent is concerned but quite unordinary in terms of their spirit and life satisfaction. One does not have to have the talent of Cezanne in order to enjoy painting. Few with a camera will capture the essence of the hills like Adams or a face like Mortensen. These four persons are now infinitely more perceptive about beauty, more aware of color, form, and design, and more appreciative of nature because they became involved in creative efforts. They have enriched every day with significant new ways to be companionable with each other and with new friends. They supplied exactly what was missing in those marriages that both Blood and Wolfe and Pineo (research sociologist who did the follow-up study on Burgess-Wallin's study of engagement and marriage) described as disenchanted, and disenchanted because companionship was lacking.

These are good cases to present because they show rather simply the way curiosity and creativity transform disillusionment into enchantment. One could have told the story of a middle-aged widow who found the same satisfaction (and later a husband) by renewing her earlier interest in drama; or of a couple who became interested in very early recordings, now have a prized collection of Galli-Curci and Kreisler, and are deeply involved in the musical world; or of another couple who at middle age went to the desert simply because of boredom, and had a hair-raising experience there with an unidentified flying object, and since have had a lively interest in that subject. There are unlimited numbers of intriguing areas of interest and new developments, such as computers, interplanetary travel, the laser beam, mental telepathy, to involve any couple for the next thousand years. It takes neither capital nor training to become engaged in significant learning. Sometimes adult education courses, university extension courses, informal discussion groups, interest groups, and training centers may help, but curiosity and comprehension must exist. Then when one is involved and working, there is creativity.

I want to be very clear about this process because no great rewards come to the dilettante who may in desultory fashion pick up *The Hobbit* because it happens to be the rage at the nearest university and a good friend chuckled over it.

A middle-aged man found that one of his friends would no longer play golf or discuss books with him—and little wonder. Every golf swing for him is an expression of his hostility at the dirty deal God gave him when he turned fifty. His score is his measure of self-esteem, and causes him to swear and rage. If he reads at all it is to maintain his self-image. He thinks he *must,* but has no zest or enthusiasm about it. He is never free to enjoy the green grass on which he is walking, the companionship of a good friend, or the occasional bird singing in a tree on the fairway. He does not hear the bird or his friend, or see the grass. There is only one honest thing to say to such a person, and his friend said it to him some time ago in declining his invitation to play a new course: that he did not need that hour on the fairway nearly as much as he needed an hour with a therapist. If one is so bound up within oneself that activities, friends, books, and nature are meaningless, then the first step ought to be in the direction of a therapist's office. Life is transformed for some individuals when they have reawakened the curiosity of their youth, gained new comprehensions about current life, and become creative as citizens or persons, but others have such a high anxiety level that no activity or interest or accomplishment will alter their conviction that life is a bad deal. They have such chains of fear and resentment that they cannot look up at the stars or identify with a character in a book. They first need therapy, and it is honest to recommend to such troubled persons the pursuit of perspective. When they have that they will be free enough to discover the horizons of contemporary life. Every reader has to make this judgment for himself. If all his good intentions and wide reading still leave him a crippled partner he ought to call a psychiatrist or marriage counselor the moment he becomes aware of the depth of his problem. If the lift of the mountains and the smell of the wave do not lift his spirits; if the smile of the child leaves him cold; if his wife's need finds him unresponsive, then he should be off for help. Therapy may have made too many people dependent on the counseling office. Members of my staff know that they get approbation from me when they report that they have helped someone to become independent and to leave. Therapists as professionals ought to pray each day to work themselves out of a job. But, having said that, I also must add that almost half of our clients are middle-aged persons who are so wounded by life, so afraid of age, so imcompetent in social interaction that they need help to become free . . . indeed just to become.

Compassion

Just to describe a person as free and as having a sense of self-worth does not mean that he has achieved full self-actualization. One would want to add to *curiosity,* which pushes us beyond our present limited vision, to *comprehension,* which enables us to know enough about things novel to *us,* and to *creativeness,* which assumes capacity to make contributions of significance, the fourth dimension of *compassion*, which makes our contributions relevant to other persons. Arthur Jersild, a most creative psychologist, described *compassion* as "the ultimate and most meaningful expression of emotional maturity."[11] It is more than understanding in that it involves feeling what another person feels. Jersild speaks of a "fellowship of feelings." When one feels compassion he is not just sympathetic; he is entering into the experiences of others. But because being truly compassionate involves emotional maturity, one can be helpful to the person with whom one is involved. One feels as he does, but is not limited as he is. One can feel with him the depth of his fear, but not be afraid oneself. Because of a closeness to the other person based on experiencing his emotion, one may give strength and be accepted by him.

To be compassionate is to experience the achievement of "withness"; it is to be so locked into a dialogue with others that nothing can disturb that communion. It results in an extraordinary fusion between persons that has great healing powers. But it is healing only if the one has sufficient emotional maturity to feel deeply the hurts of the other while being also sensitized to the futility of the way those feelings paralyze the other. He then begins to move that relationship to sounder ground. He can do this because if the other senses his sympathetic understanding the other can trust, and through trust he can venture.

Consider the relationship of a six-year-old who must go to the hospital for a tonsillectomy. He is so disturbed by the threat of this experience that each time the date approaches he develops a fever and the date is canceled. His mother is not compassionate if she permits this behavior to continue; she is being controlled. She is compassionate if she says to him:

Johnny, those tonsils are very bad. They are making you lose much time in school and eventually they could make you sicker, so they must come out. Each time we try to take you to the hospital you get sick. Next week we are going to the hospital, and if you get a fever we will wait there until you get over it.

She has taken the first step by a clear comprehension of what the situation is. She has not yet been creative or compassionate, but she goes on:

> I know that you have never been in a hospital and you are frightened. You don't quite know what is going to happen, and that is frightening. You don't know the doctor very well and that worries you. But Mother and Daddy had their tonsils out and so did your sister. It is going to be all right. And Mother or Daddy will be with you almost all the time.

What has the mother added? She has not only helped Johnny bring his fears to the surface and look at them, but she has assured him that everything will be all right despite his forebodings because everyone goes to the hospital. She has begun to help Johnny do unpleasant things with courage. She has given him a model by helping him face fear. She has also responded to his fear by saying that Mother and Daddy will be there. With this kind of support Johnny is not likely to develop a fever. But even if he does, he will have still grown a great deal.

This kind of constructive feeling *with* someone is not possible for the person who is so anxious that his own needs prevent meaningful response to another. It is not possible for power-hungry individuals who use the weaknesses of others for self-aggrandizement of their egos. It is not possible for weak persons who doubt themselves so much that they cannot bring strength where strength is needed. The intervention of one person in the life of another or in a group is healing only when there is enough openness for one to comprehend the other and be creative. Then one authenticates his right to contribute by the responsibility of his response.

The achievement of compassion is paramount for the middle-aged man and woman if they are to move meaningfully among their peers. We live in a lonely and harsh urban world. Those we have loved have gone on separate pathways that lead away from us. The environment and social situation seem to maximize deprivation of our need for closeness. In addition, the reflective person who approaches the mid-point in his years is often battered by the awareness of the absurdity of life. Before that time he was so busy struggling that he did not take stock. At mid-point he suddenly recognizes that he has just begun to develop capacity to enjoy life, he is only now free enough to think and look and listen, but now the end of it all looms ahead. The greater his involvement with life, the more poignant may be his sense of the futility of it all. He has borne the "slings and arrows of outrageous fortune" and for what? To die. He has learned finally to listen with rapture to a symphony or the wind near a river in the wilderness, but soon he will hear nothing, and forever and forever the wind will be still for him. As Maxwell Anderson, the dramatist, put it, there will be only memories of him and after awhile these too will fade. It will be as though he never existed. So he finds no meaning in his past or his future. Every twinge of pain or sense of fatigue is a reminder that tomorrow he will be no more.

The existentialists have reported these feelings of ultimate frustration more adequately than the psychologists. There is great honesty in their facing up to the dilemma. When Albert Camus pictures man's plight in the *Myth of Sisyphus*,[12] he compares him to that mythological figure forever condemned to push a great boulder to the top of a mountain, only to have it cascade down again and again. Camus' final word is that utter honesty in the acceptance of that futility is the only meaning life can have. This is a courageous stance, but certainly not the only one. There are two other kinds of experience that seem more rewarding than Camus' majestic and brave resignation.

One who has compassion attempts always to help the other push the boulder up the mountain. Many times he is not permitted to put his shoulder to the other person's boulder, but he can experience with the other his fatigue and utter a word of encouragement. He can bring water when the sun is hot and a towel to wipe off sweat. In theory perhaps it is enough for Sisyphus to push his rock to the heights, but in reality this is not so because he becomes discouraged and tired and lonely. It is only when compassion enables us to share the absurdities of existence that they become bearable and even pleasant. Camus says that the "rock is his thing." But it really is not. The rock is the property and the lot of all men and it is evil to suppose that any single person ought to bear the whole burden. The absurdity of life is less destructive when men share one another's burdens. In taking stock, as all men must do at the mid-point when decisions for the rest of life are made, one also has to answer the question of how he is to evaluate his efforts when the time for the final pause arrives.

The man who has been kind to his children, to his friends, to his parents, and to strangers will have less futility than the egocentric one who has cared only for himself.

Beyond their personal expressions of compassion for those about them, men and women who invest some of their kindly concern in social melioration leave an immortal heritage as part of the social fabric. The way the white man treats the black, the relationship of the generations, the rewards that come from the ways of intimacy between a man and a woman are not eternally fixed in either prejudice or ignorance. Life is always in flux and each one of us influences slightly *forever* the patterns of tomorrow, both by modeling and by tuition. He may do this only by his vote, or by his work in a cancer laboratory, or in a sociological survey, or in a lay board supporting all those efforts, but he is not powerless. He can help determine for tomorrow the ways in which the boulders are to be pushed toward the heights. The boulder may run down again. The next generation may have to begin all over again on a new mountain, but something is added by the creative efforts of compassionate men that cannot be lost. The something has both a technological and a humane aspect. Both are rewarding.

Commitment

Beyond that utter honesty of Camus there is this aspect of a final dimension, which is that of commitment. Camus ends with "lucid indifference"; we suggest that the rewards are greater with involved commitment.

It is this type of searching analysis that seems to be the essence of the contribution religion can make to the plight of middle-aged man. Complaining to God about fate and asking for some divine manipulation to ease the paradox of life produces little but disillusionment with faith. The curious and creative searcher is rarely a cynic. As he unravels the wonders of the world he is more often reverent than indifferent. He may be perplexed about the Creator but he feels no great need to plan his funeral. Such a man recognizes that he is only at the edge of truth and that "more truth is to be revealed" about the universe. Meantime he finds inspiration in the deepest religious thinking of the past and in the contemporary dialogue about the meaning of existence. It is enough to be a searcher and to experience the rewards of the search.

The remainder of this chapter is devoted to an analysis of the way in which *comprehension, creativeness,* and *compassion* may bridge the gaps that are isolating middle-aged men and women from those both younger and older than themselves. Part of the isolation and loneliness of the mid-years comes because of the loss of contact with adolescents on the one hand and with aging parents on the other. The conflicts between the generations are so grave that only the most sensitive approach can moderate them. Our goal is to contribute to the growth of meaningful communication with both those who are younger and those who are older.

THE GENERATIONAL GAP WITH TEEN-AGERS

Recently a group of highly successful professional men gathered just outside Chicago for a weekend of sensitivity training, for which I was sharing the leadership. The focus of the meeting was not much different from that of a great many other such gatherings of middle-aged, bored successes; they talked about the strains in their marriages, the strains in their professions, and their reactions to strain in the world. It was a strenuous weekend. But it did differ in one respect. Several of the lawyers and doctors present had sons who had graduated from Harvard, or were in the process of doing so. When the group finally departed from the melancholy recital of marital strains and chanced onto the subject of adolescents, the whole room became charged. Somehow Harvard had become responsible for a whole new subversive movement in America. One of the men bitterly recited statistics which revealed that in the previous year's class the majority of the students had chosen to work for the Peace Corps or VISTA, or had elected to pursue some type of humanitarian endeavor instead of flying back to become junior partner in Father's law office or medical facility. From that moment on, the weekend was devoted to an excoriation of this generation of youth, their lack of appreciation of our heritage, their false values, their vocabulary, goals, and personalities.

As it happened, I had just spent a week as a guest at one of the midwestern colleges with the special assignment of dialogue with the students about their values, personality problems, goals, and relationship with their parents. At the college I had listened to both individuals and groups of students as they excoriated my generation for our false values, superficiality, hypocrisy, and materialism. During that week I had utilized what skill I had in group dynamics and what truth I possessed to modify the impression youth had of their parents' generation.

But this book is directed to the parents of the older adolescents and young adults so that my position is frankly reversed and aimed at contributing some comprehension about the youth scene today. If one is successful in doing that, it is to be hoped that parents can deal more creatively with their problematical relationships with their sons and daughters. Before the discussion is over it will be obvious that compassion and commitment are also necessary if we are to narrow the "generational gap."

In the first place one ought to recognize that our teen-agers are as diverse a group as their parents. The teen-age generation, if put on a scale like one measuring the temperature of water from very cold to very hot, would vary from the hippies, who have completely dropped out, to the other end of the scale where other adolescents are completely involved in society. The hippies, the motorcycle groups, and some others have so rejected the society of their parents that they have established new communities with new laws and new social forms. On the other end of the scale are those who are equally unhappy with the acquisitive society but who prefer to remain in contact and try to modify those aspects of our heritage that they find repugnant. In the center of the scale between these groups are the great hosts of the "dead ones," those who are indifferent to anything but their own egocentric goals. But even some of these self-centered youth have adopted some of the attitudes of the "out" groups, and will continue to do so as long as those attitudes fit their drive for personal satisfaction. Thus they accept the new sexual morality, but not the "drug scene." They have not dropped out, but they have never been "in" in the sense of effective confrontation with life.

Several sociological studies have carefully defined the attitudes of the more radical wing of this generation. To comprehend why it is difficult for parents to accept new attitudes of "dropouts" one has only to see that these attitudes are rejections of the values of the last generation; J. I. Simmons and Barry Winograd, of the University of California at Santa Barbara, start defining the new point of view as being *irreverent*.[13] They reject Christianity in favor of Oriental mysticism; they want the right to evaluate the ethics of the Vietnam war, and will not accept others' judgments about it; they are greatly concerned with love, but it makes no difference whether that love is found in marriage or before marriage; they question the ethics and value of materialistic acquisition as the goal of life; they are especially critical of parents, professors, and paternalistic government. Consequently they are often unconventional and sarcastic about parental conservatism. They counter their irreverence toward the Establishment by their insistence on *humanism*, their concern for human beings and life as the final good per se. The largest group of youth who are intent on accumulation have little of this. They do not march in protest or organize for change, although a few of them at the far end of the scale of political conservatism are quite verbal about returning to yesterday.

Also characteristic of most young people today is their search for *experience*, in which they seek "the richness of life." In this they have much in common with the existentialists. They are also described as *spontaneous* and *tolerant*, but this applies mostly to the hippy group. A minority will spontaneously try anything from drugs to art, but it is unfair to generalize on the number who do. Simmons and Winograd stress the fact that they are liberal in their views, but there are just as many other adolescents who are extremely conservative. Whatever they are, they have a common honesty about it. They dislike sham and pretense. And they feel that parents, professors, Presidents, and mostly all adults are "not altogether honest, wise or competent to run the world and give advice . . ."

If parents are to talk with this generation, they have to recognize why they have such feelings of outrage against the teen-agers. It is not difficult to see why most parents would resent the irreverence of youth about the Establishment. Parents bet their lives on the values of the Establishment. Those values are central in giving direction and guidance. If young people not only reject those values but also drop out of a society based on them, they are in a very real sense saying to their parents that they gave their lives to inferior and worthless things. That's hard to take. But parents' indignation at the rejection of their values is probably secondary to their anxiety about the outcome of the younger generation's experimentation. They worry about the new sexual freedom because they are afraid their children will have to marry prematurely and they are not sure what such freedom will do to later marriage. They worry about the drugs because they do not know what physical or psychological damage the drugs will do. They worry about the economic future of their offspring because they do not feel that the Peace Corps or VISTA or Haight-Ashbury is a very auspicious beginning for financial security. Many parents stay up nights because of real fear that their adolescents will end up in jail or in automobile or motorcycle catastrophes. Not a few parents worry egocentrically that their young people will bring dishonor on the family name. Some of these worries are generated by misunderstanding, some by dismay, some by love, and others by pure selfishness. Parents need to be as honest with themselves as possible if they are going to comprehend what they are contributing to the gap between themselves and their young.

Of course some of the worry about the teen-agers comes directly from troubled memories the parents have of their own peccadilloes. They remember that they themselves were not chaste in their youth, that they cheated on examinations; some remember that they, too, defied the law during Prohibition with alcohol stolen from the chemistry lab or wine made in bathtubs and basements. They have a vague uneasiness that some of their own extramarital venturings are being reflected in the new sexual freedom of youth, and this they find difficult to face. When their children reprove them for archaic attitudes toward race relations they grow angry because they have long been uneasy about those attitudes themselves. Part of the debris of the broken bridges between the middle-aged and their teen-agers or young adults is the guilt of the older generation. Some fathers are aware that there is some merit in the rejection of the acquisitive attitude by youth because they themselves were neglected by parents who spent most of their time at work when their children were growing up and not with the family.

Edgar Z. Friedenberg, a well-known educator from Brooklyn, adds another insight which is very germane to a book on the middle years. He says that one of the large factors in the alienation of parent and child is the parent's fear and resentment of aging:

> It is not paradox, certainly, that people who are determined to stay young should resent people who actually are young. . . . Young people, who really do have their lives ahead of them, and who have not yet begun in earnest to make the least of their opportunities, are bound to arouse mixed feelings in their elders.[14]

In this sense, part of the hostility of parents to youth has little to do with the extravagances of today's adolescents. It rests again in the unwillingness of parents to accept the aging process.

In summary, the rejection by many of our young people of our way of life combines with our reaction to their rejection (our sensing it as a threat to our ordered existence; our honest worry about the consequences of their behavior to those we love; and our unwillingness to acknowledge our own guilts, together with our panic over aging) to determine our quick and hostile reaction to the adolescent we wish would vanish. Until we are familiar with our own motives, we cannot be objective in moving towards a new rapprochement with our children. Anger, denunciation, haughty and imperialistic advice-giving will not bridge the gap. Worry and anxiety will help not at all. Complaining only intensifies the distance between us. What is needed is that openness of mind and heart we have called *compassion*. This implies a willingness to be so close to and so *with* our young people that we can understand why they have to reject our world or withdraw from it. When they sense our compassion they will move towards us, for most of them are as lost as we were at that age. Their "love-ins" are desperate efforts to find some intimacy lost to the modern world. Their withdrawal from the rat race may be, in some measure, the pioneering of an age of technology when the Calvinistic worship of work will no longer be relevant. They are the victims of an awesome change in society which we never faced and with which we would probably have coped with equal trouble had it happened to us. In the face of that world, they too are afraid and in need of the guidance and support of the more experienced. But they will not buy it with penitence and conformity. They will accept it from others who accept them.

THE GENERATIONAL GAP WITH THE ELDERLY

There is much concentration on the difficulty in communication between adolescents and parents, but if one has the opportunity, as I do, to sit with groups of middle-aged persons, he soon discovers that they are equally troubled by their relationships with their own elderly parents. The separation between these two generations is extreme in many cases, and its roots are as important as those of the separation with youth.

The gap between the middle-aged and their elderly parents has been noted by several researchers. In analyzing material for a paper on the motivational aspects of housing for the elderly, I paid particular attention to the sources of advice and counsel used by those considering a move. Less than 20 per cent of the subjects had turned to their middle-aged children for help in making this significant decision. Marvin Sussman did an important study of the relationships of married children to their parents and discovered that in general there is little sharing of advice between the generations.[15] What contact is there? Both Sussman and Eugene Litwak, a prominent sociologist, think that a network of help is present so that if those who wanted to move had stringent financial problems their sons and daughters would do what they could to help them balance their budget. If the parents were ill, their children would come to their aid. My respondent subjects said that under no circumstances would they ever live with their married sons or daughters. They like to see them occasionally but not too often, and they like to have their grandchildren around once in awhile. There is no evidence that much of a primary (face-to-face) closeness is left in these relationships.

This separateness of parents and their married children produces a great amount of guilt in the children. In conference and after conference they say something like this:

> But I don't know what to do with mother. She is so lonely, but whenever she's at our house there's so much tension that we can't stand it. Of course I love her . . . it's just that I don't want her interfering in our

lives. Whenever I do see her she complains that I never get there. I hate to send her to an old folks' home but I guess there's no alternative.

Seemingly in American society there is no other alternative. Only 2 per cent of married children have their parents living with them. A whole industry is developing to house and nurse our retired parents. Society is beginning to provide much better housing, medical care, and activities for the twenty million people in our country who are over fifty-five. But this does not help the middle-aged son and daughter who have been told to "honor thy father and thy mother." They have a profound conflict between feeling that they *should* take them into their home, that they *should* spend a great deal of time with them, and the other feeling that they do not want to do so.

The reaction of the middle-aged person is compounded of a series of profound psychological reactions. There is role reversal, which consists of the involution of relationships. As our parents become older they lose confidence in their own judgment; consequently they become dependent. When we are called upon to be parents to them we have trouble reversing our attitudes. This need for us to be ascendant and authoritative often brings to the surface all the old hostilities that were generated for the twenty years when they were in control. We therefore vaguely resent the need to be kind and helpful to those who controlled us previously. We likewise find it difficult to teach those whose primary role earlier was to teach us. Another strand in the difficulty is the demand on our time. Our chief focus is on work and our own nuclear families, and to have to deal with those who are "retired" from life is onerous to us. Furthermore, there is much misunderstanding because our values have changed considerably from those which moved us when we were adolescents. We are impatient with the world in which our parents move. Beyond this is the fact that we sense things have changed between our fathers and mothers. They, too, have reversed roles. As Mother grows older she takes command, and is indeed very demanding. Father is not the strong, self-reliant person we knew when we were growing up and this bothers us. Now he is retiring, submissive, and gentle. He makes adaptations to life by adjusting to his inner self, and this is out of character for us. We are annoyed and confused by these changes, and this complicates our response to their need now to be dependent on us. Finally, we are annoyed because contact with our parents reminds us that in a few years we too must pass through this period of growing dependence, and we do not like to be reminded of that fact.

It is difficult to sort out our feelings about our parents, but it is imperative to do so if we are to resolve the guilt that many of us carry about the relationship. There is no substitute again for honesty in terms of all the things we feel. Once we have acknowledged our own hesitations and hostilities, we can begin to listen to our parents and understand what needs they have and what we may do about it. Age is not honored in our society, and many sons and daughters contribute to their parents' loss of self-esteem. But if we listen to them we can understand that they really do not ask much. If we share what we can realistically in time and love, life will be richer for us and for them. Again, the practice of compassion heals the gap.

SUMMARY

Making the most of middle age may be seen now as living on intellectual, aesthetic, and social frontiers. Beyond this is the need to draw into our circle once more both those we raised and those who raised us. There is a fearful loss when children and parents are somehow alienated from us. To reconstitute the whole family is difficult because in one sense we have to live in tomorrow and in another we have to understand yesterday, but with compassion and commitment this is possible. It has already been suggested that the same type of tenderness and involvement is essential if we are to rescue our marriages from mediocrity and gradual alienation. All of this involves broader focus of life and some new honesty about ourselves and our past relationships. We cannot evade stock-taking; but if that stock-taking is positive, middle age can indeed be the prime of life.

7

Anticipation
of
Things
to Come

If the loss of children precipitates a crisis in family life, there is another to follow which must be faced by all men. The work life is one day over and retirement confronts the man who has organized his last forty years around his occupation. This change inevitably creates still another problem of adjustment for both husband and the wife.

THE CRISIS AT RETIREMENT

The end of a work career brings with it a number of role shocks. One of the most severe is the readjustment of the relationship of husband and wife, who have become used to seeing each other a limited number of hours a day. Some marriages persist only because opportunity for contact is limited. When the partners in such marriages face continuous confrontation, misery results. Another role shock has to do with the sudden end of enforced routine, with the new freedom to invest one's efforts in one's own way, with the relief from the tensions and demands associated with any career. But with this shock comes another, for the end of the occupation means the swift reduction in financial resources and generally a change in status.

All of these may serve to confuse both the man and his wife, say gerontologists Wilma Donahue, Harold Orback, and Otto Pollack, and to produce a "shock effect on the physiology and personality organization of the individual."[1] They conclude that this presents a "major challenge" to all the individual's resources. The disorganizing aspects of this crisis will be less if "the individual has taken anticipatory measures."[2] Thus the ideal time to prepare for retirement is in those years of middle age when a couple have the time and resources to plan effectively for their last years.

In one sense the need for anticipatory planning for an older age may make a significant contribution to middle-age adjustment. If individuals take the long view that middle age provides more leisure time and more freedom than the period of child raising, then the development of interests which will make the retirement years significant also cushions the transition experienced in the child-launching period. Every person's life is at all times incomplete and fragmentary in terms of the totality of his wishes and needs. If he utilizes the mid-years to take some steps in the expansion of life space by cultivating new friends, new mental horizons, new interests, he has provided that type of foundation which makes the advent of retirement less of a shock than it might otherwise have been. We are suggesting that planning may well be for the last half of life and not simply for middle age or, later, for old age. If couples do make such enlargements, they will certainly benefit both periods.

ROLE REVERSAL

The emphasis here has been on couples because we have already suggested some knotty developments that plague couples with retirement. The suggestions regarding role reversal between husband and wife may be normal for most couples, but they are not at all inevitable. Certainly the turbulence that such role reversal occasions can be rather completely avoided when the husband and wife are aware of the nature of those changes.

Why does the wife become domineering and the husband submissive? Part of the explanation is probably endocrinological. The wife loses more and more of her estrogenic hormones that influence her feminine behavior and produces more testosterone. The husband on the other hand is constantly producing less testosterone. From a psychological point of view there is the whole reaction formation on the part of the wife to the fear of disruption of her habits and household management by a husband who is now going to be underfoot all the time.

A woman once said to me when I was interviewing her on the television show, "Houseparty": "I don't know what has gotten into my husband. All our lives he was content. Now that he is home he complains all the time that I am a rotten housekeeper. Why is that?" I had to explain to her that "This is the first time he really has had a look at your housekeeping, and could know how bad you are!" After that facetious remark I went on to explain that the man was not really complaining about her housekeeping. He was merely expressing his irritation at his own unemployment and lack of things to do. Many women steel themselves for the moment when their husbands are going to be permanently home. There is a sociological aspect, too, in the sudden drop of status when a man leaves work. Hitherto he has earned his place in the family as the provider. What is he when he quits work? He contributes little. It is true that a couple live because he earned and saved, but his main function as the instrumental leader is gone. It is perhaps precisely because of this that his wife now becomes the leader and he recedes into the background. In many families this reversal of role leads to disastrous quarreling and unhappiness. But such a catastrophic conclusion to a lifetime of togetherness does not have to happen. If a couple have, at middle age, taken the opportunity afforded by that transition to build new communication and to develop new ways of sharing, by the time they reach retirement these patterns will be well established and no great new adjustment will need to be made or damage suffered.

MARITAL ADJUSTMENT—THE CRITICAL ISSUE

One of the most significant insights which has come from the series of cases studied by Otto Pollack, a prominent sociologist and gerontologist, is that marital adjustment is the critical issue. For instance he found that no activity, no matter how engaging and rewarding, contributes to good adjustment in aging unless it is accepted by the marital partner.

> The increased importance of the marriage relationship in this phase of life makes harmony with the spouse apparently a *conditio sine qua non* of positive adjustment.[3]

This comment means far more to us than simply a comment on retirement interests. It highlights the increasing significance of good marital relationships for life satisfaction as the years pass. It is a common finding of all gerontological studies that marital pairs are far happier than individuals who are single, widowed, or divorced. Again the significance of this fact for middle-aged persons is obvious. If, at the critical juncture of the prime of life, behavior is such as to sow seeds of suspicion or to infer neglect of the other, the deterioration of the relationship will have disastrous results later on in life. On the other hand, the couple who at this point in time renew their vows of fidelity and concern lay an important foundation for the type of union that is decisive for later happiness. When I have urged attention in great earnestness to new emphasis on marriage I have been also discussing preparation for success during the retirement years. Couples who renew their concern for their marriages will still have adjustments to make when the husband's work role is over, but they will know few of the calamitous repercussions experienced by those who have been increasingly alienated during the middle years.

PREPARING TO BE THE ELDERLY PARENTS

There are other relationships which need attention during the middle years if there is to be a payoff later on. In the last chapter we discussed both the need to bridge the generational gap with sons and daughters and the problems of dealing with parents. But not far in the future is the time when we will be the elderly parents and our present adolescents and young adults will be middle-aged. They too will face the problems with us that we are facing with our parents! We too, in need of some warmth from them, will resent their lack of attention and concern. But the resolution of this problem can also be made in this period if we can transcend our growing rigidity and make the rapprochement with our young people suggested in the last chapter. *Much of the difficulty between middle-aged persons and their parents is the final statement of their failure to work out closeness earlier in life.*

THE NEED FOR RECOGNITION

Pollack also discovered that the need for recognition, or "social approval," increases with age. Having given up the prime method for gaining approval in our society—working—the retired person covets acceptance. For instance, individuals who had taken up a new interest, such as painting, want to see their works admired. Recently when I had finished a lecture outlining in detail all the ways retired persons could enjoy new activities, one man expressed the group's response: "That's all very good, Dr. Peterson, but what can we do that has *meaning* to others. We don't simply want to amuse ourselves."

Those activities encountered in the middle years that bring one into close contact with others and that can be continued until the end of life are more apt to be useful to the ego than some novel concern developed after retirement. By retirement, one ought to have some skill and some achievement in the interest so that he is not defeated in trying a new pursuit for the first time. It is this continuity of at least part of a person's life that prohibits him from that "roleless role" described by Ernest Burgess, a top sociologist at the University of Chicago.

FINANCIAL SECURITY

Retirement is unattractive only to those who have not learned the "equivalence of work and play" or who have not already established competence in the leisure arts, provided that they can afford it.

Provided that they can afford it—this is one of the critical determinants of adjustment in the later years. The possibility of travel, hobbies, adequate housing, visiting family, and health care are all dependent on whether the man who has left his job has provided sufficient means to live well. Whether he will be comfortable or not in his retirement years depends on the skill with which he previously planned his financial life.

The life cycle presents different financial demands at each stage. It is one of the ironies of our system that the period of maximum expense in bearing and raising and educating children usually comes before a man has reached his maximum earning capacity. Furthermore, most families in America are buying a home and making other payments constantly while they are in these earlier phases of earning capacity. By the time a man is earning his maximum, his home may be paid for and his children through college. He has fifteen years or more of employment to go at maximum pay and lower expenses. While he should have been saving some all along, this is the period when he can make maximum investments for his retirement.

Al and Susan illustrate a life cycle financial plan geared to the differential demands of different needs in their life together. When they were first married, they put off child bearing for three years and saved all of her salary to make a down payment on a home, to pay off their automobiles, and to lay aside money for doctor bills and hospital expenses when she became pregnant. They conscientiously added one bit of furniture after another to the nursery until at the end of three years their room for the baby was ready; so was their savings account. In the meantime Al carried term insurance, which was the cheapest he could buy. When Susan quit work, they did not need to reduce their living habits because they had been living on his salary.

During the next fifteen years they consistently raised the amount of insurance they carried and every year invested in a savings bond and a mutual fund program so that when their first child was ready for college a generous sum was available. At the time their second child entered college, the twenty-year mortgage on their house was paid off and they were able to divert some of the income that had been used for those payments to ease the strain caused by having two children in college. With payments eased, normal increments in salary, and the use of savings designated for educational expenditures, they were able to maintain three children in college and still live well.

When the last child graduated from college, they entered the third phase of their economic plan. They then invested for their retirement the income they had previously used as payments on their home and for the children's education. They also began to enlarge their interests by investing in photographic equipment, extension courses, and a program of travel, which they had carefully planned in earlier years. Travel was possible because they had more means and Al had earned longer and longer vacations due to his increasing years with his company. But programs change and needs sometimes take sudden turns. On a trip to Mexico this particular couple became greatly intrigued with the early history of that country, and they longed to spend a good deal of time in exploring the excavation of early pyramids and towns. As they could not afford this, Susan decided to go back to work for several years to provide them a longer "sabbatical" in Mexico. Like hundreds of thousands of other middle-aged women, she found that employment was available and that she enjoyed the work. At the end of three years Al was granted a leave, and they made their expedition. Susan's salary, as it had been in the first years of marriage, was carefully earmarked for these special goals, and their savings program for the future was not impaired.

By the time they were ready for retirement they had accumulated sufficient funds to enable them to carry on their lives in a rewarding way.

Financial planning for retirement is often superficial because the couple asks the wrong questions. It is not enough to save money to sustain life: to pay the rent, insurance policies, clothing, food, and other necessities. The wise person will accumulate enough to provide, beyond the necessities, for (1) underwriting those hobbies, travel plans, books, etc., which are essential for a full life, and (2) any large catastrophic event, such as a fire, long illness, or injury to a loved one, that may occur. No scale has ever been devised which would help families in specifically anticipating their future needs because each couple have grossly different needs. Nevertheless many hours of discussion and pencil work will pay large dividends in contentment later on in life. It is now obvious that middle age is the time when these concerns become a paramount interest and when there is a real opportunity to implement them.

In looking at retirement income there are some specific facts which can be recorded. The income from Social Security can be projected with fair accuracy. The income from a company retirement program can be ascertained without difficulty. Income from savings and loan accounts can be estimated within certain limits. The income from stocks and bonds is not so easily estimated because their value fluctuates from year to year. However the value of money in banks and savings and loan associations or in retirement funds tends to become less because of inflation, while money invested in real estate or stocks and bonds rises as the market rises. The Federal Government has tried to introduce a compensatory program to inflation by raising Social Security payments to match the decrease of dollar value. Probably a varied type of savings and retirement investment which considers both safety and hedges against inflation is the wisest course. Some retirement programs now split their investments between straight savings, on the one hand, and stocks and bonds, on the other. This field is more complex than it may appear to an average husband and wife so that taking a course in investments or employing an investment counselor would be an intelligent way to make retirement investment sound and safe.

The retirement income of retired persons shows some improvement, but not much. The following table is included, not for academic reasons, but to emphasize the seriousness of our recommendation that middle-aged persons plan diligently for their future. This table is adapted from one put out by the Administration on Aging, of the Department of Health, Education and Welfare, and summarizes the latest available data.

Some 23 per cent, or about one fourth, of the families whose head was over the age of sixty-five had an income of less than $2,000 a year; 10 per cent had an income over $10,000 a year. The plight of

TABLE II

Trends in Median Family Income[4]

| | FAMILIES | | | | |
| | Head 14–64 | | Head 65 and over | | |
YEAR	Amount	Per Cent Change	Amount	Per Cent Change	Per Cent of 14–64
1960	$5,905	%	$2,897	%	%
1961	6,099	3.3	3,026	4.4	49.1
1962	6,336	3.9	3,204	5.9	49.6
1963	6,644	4.9	3,352	4.6	50.6
1964	6,981	5.1	3,376	0.7	50.4
1965	7,352	5.3	3,460	2.5	47.1

single persons over sixty-five was greater because one third of them had incomes of less than $1,000 and 57.9 per cent had incomes of less than $1,500. If we consider that a person or a family (where both parents work) earns on the average today $7,353 a year for forty years, almost $300,000 will have passed through a typical checking account by the time retirement arrives. Careful budgeting should make it possible to add enough to Social Security and company retirement plans to prevent impairment of plans for a full and happy involvement during the retirement years. This is primarily a middle-age task.

KEEPING HEALTHY

Of course money does not alter the fact of aging and it cannot buy freedom from the aches and pains of our last years; 80 per cent of our current population sixty-five and over report one or more chronic health condition or impairments. Still, half of these report that these conditions do not impose any limitations on their activities, but one out of five (20 per cent) report that they are unable to carry on what they designate as their major activity at all. Of those older persons who report that impairments do limit their activities, the most frequently reported problems are heart conditions (21.8 per cent), arthritis and rheumatism (20.7 per cent), and visual impairment (9.5 per cent). Thirty-six per cent of all persons in the middle-age group of ages fifty-five to sixty-four have lost all of their permanent teeth. This figure goes up to 56 per cent by ages sixty-five to seventy-four. Evidence is fairly conclusive that a great many individuals are not enjoying optimum health because of dental deficiencies. Mental illness reaches its peak during the middle-age period of ages thirty-five to fifty-five and then declines. The total number of commitments to mental hospitals increases after fifty-five through seventy because of the large number of older persons who suffer from cerebral arteriosclerosis and senile psychosis. The incidence of the psychosis falls rapidly during the period fifty-five and older.

It has been said that there are no diseases of old age. What occurs to the cells and tissues then is the direct result of insults to them throughout the course of life by disease, malnutrition, and neglect. We have suggested that death rates in the United States for the forty-to-sixty age group appear higher than in almost any other country. Remember that part of this may simply mean that the science of medicine has already added many years to the lives of those who in other cultures would be dead much earlier. But it may also be a product of our "good living," in which we can afford to eat and drink too much. Whatever the cause, more adequate care would reduce mortality. What can be done during middle age to make those years more comfortable and to lay a foundation for a relatively healthy old age?

Dental care is one of the most important factors. During middle age much of the problem resides in pyorrhea and other diseases of the gums and mouth. Cavities do not pose such an important problem as overall oral health. For this reason strict adherence to a program of dental inspection may mean the difference between health and poor health. If one recalls the loss of permanent teeth during and after this period and the comments about the importance of oral hygiene to general health, such a regime is indispensable.

Nutrition is of optimum importance. Poor nutrition affects both mental and physical vigor. Malnutrition may make the difference between heart compensation and heart failure. Adequate diet has been related to mental health. For middle-aged persons one might add that there is a problem not so much of malnutrition as of over-nutrition, the tendency to eat oneself to death.

A third aspect of preventive health care is the maintenance of consistent levels of exercise. Vascular tissues are almost always found to be in better condition in those who exercise. It is instructive to note that the more a diabetic exercises, the less supportive insulin he needs. Most of us are acquainted with the fact that the heart specialists who have treated our Presidents have insisted that they add more than the rocking chair to their daily movements! This does not apply when the illness is far advanced. In fact all of these general recommendations are to be modified by the specific instructions of one's physician.

There is the fourth matter of preventive medicine. Long ago several surveys including thousands of subjects under scrutiny discovered that about one third of the respondents had undetected disease and that a large number of them improved under treatment. Eugene Confrey and Marcus Goldstein, students of aging, list diseases of the heart, malignant neoplasm, and vascular lesions affecting the central nervous system as accounting for three of every four deaths above the age of forty-four. They go on to relate this to middle age: "On the other hand, many of the premature deaths from disease might have been averted had appropriate preventive measures been followed."[7]

They state two cases, cancer of the uterus and obesity leading to fatal cases of heart disease, that might have been prevented by earlier care. The implication for making consistent preventive visits to the physician is evident. Middle-aged men and women can assure themselves of not only a longer but also a healthier second half of life by utilizing their medical contacts for prevention as well as cure. The proliferation of preventive immunization for influenza and other conditions is part of this program.

While the research material does not yet give a clear picture of the relationship of morale to illness, most gerontologists conclude such studies by indicating that they feel that a "sense of purpose and of continuing participation in life" is essential to good mental and physical health. No individual is just a mind, or just a physique. All of these combine in a psychosomatic way to determine morale and satisfaction. What we have indicated in these paragraphs is the critical importance of paying attention to dental, mental, and physical health in such a way that we may reap the advantages of recent and current medical research. No other course of action seems sensible when we contemplate the dividends.

DEVELOPING NEW ORGANIZATIONAL CONTACTS

While it has been suggested tangentially in earlier discussions that middle age is a period to develop new organizational contacts and experiences, it has not been talked about in detail. This enlargement of contacts is viewed in this chapter as a prerequisite to adjustment after retirement, but it has as much promise for the middle-age period as it does for the later one. We take our clue from Robert Havighurst, who says that the changes in role that are required of workers when they retire demand role flexibility and that ". . . probably the best assurance of role flexibility in later years is a reasonably successful experience in a variety of roles during the middle years, the emphasis being on *reasonable* and *variety,* for outstanding success in certain roles in middle age sometimes makes for rigidity."[9]

Some writers have felt that role flexibility can be deliberately cultivated during this middle period of life, and they have developed programs to help men and women in this period develop new interests which lead to "useful and creative roles."

The scope of opportunity for new roles in new formal and informal organizations is unlimited. One may decide either to intensify participation in religious or educational groups or to invade new fields. The critical point in decision must consider two dimensions: (1) Does this new interest contain future rewards that will be emotionally satisfying over a long period of time? (2) What opportunity does this venture provide for long-term human contact? One can collect buttons and bows or he can study the philosophy of the Greeks. He can hunt mushrooms or agates, become a deacon in his church, or take golf lessons. What seems essential is that middle-aged persons recognize this period as a pivotal time for change. "In order to build an effective program at older age levels," says J. E. Anderson, "we must build it as a new product, even though it is based on past interests and activities."[10]

It is this renewed interest in life beyond the family circle that would make the contribution and capacity of middle-aged persons available for the guidance of society. On the other hand the sense of worth and new stimulation that comes to both men and women by participation means much to them. Women in their forties tend to increase the time they give to voluntary organizations, sometimes to the extent that this becomes a major aspect of their lives. Men likewise serve as members of boards of directors or as trustees of the same groups in which their wives are active. Women participate more often than men, but that is understandable because men are more often employed. Voluntary organizations can be divided into two types: those aimed primarily at ameliorating some problem faced by society (these may serve such large purposes as those included in the Red Cross or they may be very specific in limiting their interest to a specific disease), and those which bring together individuals for the purpose of enhancing their own interests (an example would be a philatelic club where the members focus on learning about and trading stamps). Many individuals belong to both types of groups; one contributes to their sense of adding something to the common wealth and the other to the individual's specific leisure-time interests. Men find status and spiritual return in contributing their knowledge of administrative skills to worthwhile community endeavors. They may contribute through religious, political, or community groups. Whatever they do, they are laying a foundation of information and experience which will stand them in good stead in the later years when they can give more time and energy to the organization. This enables them in later years to be a part of life even though they are retired. But unless this is done during the middle years the person will not have the contacts, the interest, the skill, or the opportunity to do so later.

SUMMARY

It is now evident in discussing the relationships of the middle-aged person that whatever he does will have repercussions in the later years. He is inevitably laying the foundations for retirement during that period from forty to sixty when he has the mental and energy levels to achieve role change and to develop new interests. The way he treats his health during this period will determine his health later. The manner in which he solves his problems in relation to his spouse and his children will be mirrored in happiness or unhappiness during his last years. The wisdom of his investment program will greatly affect the scope of his opportunities in the later period of his life. His participation in an amplified group of activities and organizations will determine the richness of his experience when he is no longer working. The surprising thing is that whatever he does to insure a fuller experience in his years after work will also enrich the mid-years of his life.

8

The Choice
Is
Yours

A great many of us would not have had to face these problems a century ago. We would not have been here. Average life expectancy has increased 75 per cent in the last century. Child rearing used to extend so far into old age that the mother had no middle-age role change. The work life continued until death, and there were few opportunities for free time in middle age or leisure in old age. The work was hard and the returns few, so that neither energy nor resources existed to enjoy an expanded life style. We begin our summary with this observation because the more than thirty million today who are in this period of life ought first to be deeply grateful to medical science and to the architects of our economy for having presented us with life and the chance to make it abundant. Whether we utilize those gifts and find fulfillment or ignore them and find futility is our choice. But in struggling for growing satisfaction we ought not to lose perspective and forget our good fortune.

Perspective of another kind comes when we relate our mid-years to all the others that have come before and those that will come after. As the child is the father to the man, so is the man in his prime the source of his later and older self. Each age builds upon the learning of the past and each succeeding life era carries the scars of the days when there were tears. Each phase in the family developmental cycle has unique tasks and characteristics which furnish novel challenges and types of responses. But they are interrelated so that the man and woman in middle age carry into that period a growing sense of satisfaction with their relationship or a growing process of alienation. Work, marriage, retirement, community involvement are all social processes which, like snowballs rolling down a hill, gather meaning and weight with each layer of time that is added. To complicate the matter, the roles of those involved in the cycle are changing rapidly, and this complicates old patterns of relationships. Good adjustment implies harmonious expectations by husband and wife for each age period. Conflicting role expectations at the time of marriage may alienate couples so that by middle age their goals and communication are completely disrupted.

We have been much concerned with the identity, or sense of self-worth, that marks the man at the mid-point of his life. He is going through a marked crisis in his psychological, work, social, and sexual roles. His wife likewise has similar and at times more severe problems. He may worry about masculinity, but she knows that her reproductive life is over. He may be gray and tired, but is plagued by old and burdensome physical afflictions. A recognition of the normality and pervasiveness of these phases *before they occur* enables individuals to cope with them. Furthermore in the last decade both physical and psychological sciences have tested new treatments so that consultation now permits more comfort and better adjustment. Marital stress is unnecessary when one utilizes resources that are at hand today.

It is this failure to utilize educational or medical resources that often condemns the middle-aged person to needless ennui or physical distress. There are many health benefits to be derived from the replacement of estrogen by artificial means—the relief of hot flushes and flashes, the countering of negative changes in blood vessels, and the prevention of bone brittleness. And the opinion once held that estrogen, if used continuously, might cause cancer has been "pretty well disproved."[1]

Bernice Neugarten provides valuable insights into the reasons why women fail to utilize this new medical therapy:

> What remains now is an educational problem: to inform large numbers of women and large numbers of physicians of the benefits of estrogen replacement and to alter long-held contrary attitudes about letting nature take its course. The new information will be of maximum value if acted upon by women relatively early in their lives, that is, for the average woman, in her late 40's.[2]

The implication of these remarks is that a major breakthrough in health has yet to be shared with women through education.

So it is with many innovations that are available for enrichment of the middle years. Some persons do not reach out for enlightenment and still others refuse to try new patterns because of habit.

Equally damaging to the middle-aged man and woman are failures to develop new patterns of relationship to people occupying other levels of the family developmental cycle, their adolescents or young adults and their own parents. The sense of frustration and the deep bitterness that marks many couples' reaction to the young and to the old is poison to them and destructive of some of the great rewards that ought to come from contact in the extended family. Continued failure in those relationships leaves a permanent guilt and cleavage which will prevent closeness at and after retirement. We have tried to analyze many of these difficulties and show that they rest in the unconscious of the middle-aged person. He must have self-awareness if he is to achieve the kind of sympathetic understanding that will bridge the gap between himself and those he cares for who are both just beginning and close to ending their life span.

In the same way, one at this time of life must attend to the broadening of his friendship network because now he must rely more on friends and neighbors for intimacy than on his children. Every man and woman needs *tenderness* and *withness* but these cannot be demanded from grown children who have to share those emotions with their own growing family. Those grandchildren will be a source of delight to the middle-ager for the rest of his life if he does not alienate his married children with too many demands and if he can bridge the generational gap by working hard for rapport with them. In the meantime the middle-aged man and woman should turn to their own peers for some of the emotional responses they found before in their home. The expression of motherhood and fatherhood can be generalized to a good many unfortunates in society who are also deprived of affect and comfort. In this way men and women do not become disengaged, but simply broaden the base along which their lives move.

Their spiritual lives can grow, too, because they now have the time and the finances to vivify past interests and to create new ones. This is the time to turn to the library for those books that were missed when the husband was establishing himself in his occupation and the wife was tending all the wants of the children. It is the time to visit the museums and the parks, the forests and the cities, the relatives long neglected, and the old friend who has moved into a distant part of the city. It is the time to catch up on the march of science, the discoveries of psychology, sociology, and anthropology, to read history and poetry, plays and novels. It is the period to perfect one's skill with a camera lens, or a golf club, or a fishing fly; to learn to turn the potter's wheel or paint the favorite vacation spot. One may now have time to promote a political point of view or help the church ease its debt. New organizations can be discovered that bring fellowship with others who have similar interests or hobbies or who implement some lifetime concern. Middle age in this sense has opportunities unlimited.

A couple may find that they are so heavily committed financially due to impulsive sprees that occurred after their major obligations were over that they cannot well afford to expand their life space. They may not be aware of the need now to budget their new affluence with retirement in mind. But if this is true, it certainly is inopportune. The middle years are those in which a couple must bear in mind, not this year or the next one, but all the remaining years of the last half of life. Their financial program ought to include the achievement during middle age of the answers to unmet needs of the wife, long postponed because of other demands, and a careful provision for the total future. Included has to be some recognition that the wife will probably face a number of those years by herself. She will need services from others that the husband will not be there to provide. This implies a whole new perspective about money management, geared to a richer life now and a comfortable life in retirement.

But there are some who, because of fear of change, rigidity of role playing, anxiety about health or love, long alienation from mate or children, are simply not able to move creatively into this period. They carry too heavily the weight of past defeats in their hearts. The price of venturing has been too poignant. They are crippled. Such individuals may never know the prime of life; for them, this period will only be one of desperation and inner sorrow. But if this is true they have indeed made of the best period of life a wasteland and they have laid it waste unnecessarily. The resources of psychologists, psychiatrists, social work agencies, such as Family Service, the skill of qualified marriage counselors or family therapists are everywhere at their disposal. No person ought ever to waste a day of his life in self-pity or self-defeating anger at others. The resources of trained and dedicated experts can be his if he only asks for them. If he has few financial reserves there are very adequate community resources to serve him. How will he know where to find such help? His family doctor, his priest, minister, or rabbi, the psychology department of a local school can all advise him where to turn. In fact, many doctors and clergymen are now so well trained that he may not have to venture beyond their offices to gain a better perspective and move toward a new life course.

These constructive alternatives to despair or disenchantment in middle age prove, upon thought, to have even greater significance, for they are prophylactic as far as retirement years are concerned. Every step in improving relations with a spouse, with children, with parents, every step in the cultivation of new friends and interests also lays a foundation with people and with inner satisfactions that will serve when the mid-years are over. These steps serve also to gain comprehension and to develop creativity that will bring greater usefulness and satisfaction later on, in old age. In one sense we have discovered that the mid-years are, in truth, pivotal for all of the rest of life.

A FINAL WORD

If you are about to put down this book and your only reaction is that all this is true, this reading experience has meant little to you. An accurate perception of the way things are, even a good prescription of how they can be, means little unless one moves to implement them. The joys of intellectual searching, the warm response of new friends, taking steps toward better health, the satisfactions of time invested in a good cause are all theoretical unless one practices them. Man is the only creature that is given the power to make choices, to improve thus upon yesterday, and to level the road for tomorrow. Days for men and women do not have to be the same; they can be full of innovation and exhilaration. It is this hope that the period of life that is so disenchanting and dull for so many may change for those who read these pages that makes the effort of writing meaningful. Man does control his destiny. There is no other moment in life that is so decisive as the hours at the mid-point when he, in essence, either by neglect, by defensiveness, by denial, or by creative enterprise charts the rest of his life. Decisions for growth and specific steps toward that growth make the middle years the prime of life.

Notes

CHAPTER 1—MIDDLE-AGE CRISIS

1. Robert O. Blood, Jr., and Donald M. Wolfe, *Husbands and Wives: The Dynamics of Married Living* (New York: The Free Press of Glencoe, 1960).
2. Edmund Bergler, *The Revolt of the Middle-Aged Man* (New York: Hill & Wang, Inc., 1958).
3. C. H. Grattan, "Curiosity, Creativeness, Comprehension," in *Aging in Today's Society*, ed. Clark Tibbitts and Wilma Donahue (Englewood Cliffs, N. J.: Prentice-Hall, Inc., 1960), p. 195.
4. Robert J. Havighurst, "Middle Age—The New Prime of Life," in *ibid.*, pp. 139–45.

CHAPTER 2—REMEMBRANCE OF THINGS PAST

1. Robert J. Havighurst, *Human Development and Education* (New York: Longmans, Green & Co., 1953).
2. Lee Travis and Dorothy Baruch, *Personal Problems of Everyday Life* (New York: D. Appleton-Century Co., 1941), p. 129.
3. James A. Peterson, *Education for Marriage* (New York: Charles Scribner's Sons, 1964), p. 123.
4. Paul C. Glick, *American Families* (New York: John Wiley & Sons, Inc., 1957), pp. 55–58.
5. J. S. Slotkin, as reported by Sid Ross and Ernest La France in *Parade, July* 17, 1955, reprinted in *Aging in Today's Society*, ed. Clark Tibbitts and Wilma Donahue (Englewood Cliffs, N. J.: Prentice-Hall Inc., 1960), pp. 132-35.
6. National Manpower Council, *Womanpower* (New York: Columbia University Press, 1957).
7. Bernice Neugarten and others, *Personality in Middle and Late Life* (New York: Atherton Press, 1964).
8. Slotkin, *loc. cit.*

CHAPTER 3—ROLES IN THE FAMILY TEAM

1. Marvin Sussman, "Intergenerational Family Relationships and Social Role Changes in Middle Age," *Marriage and Family Living*, reprinted

151

in *Problems of the Aged,* comp. Clyde B. Vedder and A. S. Lefkowitz (Springfield, Ill.: Charles C Thomas, Publisher, 1965), pp. 92—100.

2. Robert O. Blood, Jr., and Donald M. Wolfe, *Husbands and Wives: The Dynamics of Married Living* (New York: The Free Press of Glencoe, 1960).

3. Adapted from *ibid.,* p. 42.

4. *Ibid.,* p. 44.

5. *Ibid.,* p. 170.

6. *Ibid.,* p. 233.

CHAPTER 4—IDENTITY CRISES AT MIDDLE AGE

1. Quoted by Art Seidenbaum in "The Man Who Dared to Unbuckle Himself From Routine," *Los Angeles Times,* August 21, 1966, p. 3.

2. William H. Masters, M.D., and M. D. Ballow, M.D., "The Third Sex," *Geriatrics,* X (June, 1955), p. 1–4.

3. Isadore Rubin, *Sexual Life After Sixty* (New York: Basic Books, Inc., 1965), p. 118.

4. Elmer Hess, M.D., Russel B. Roth, M.D., and Anthony F. Kaminsky, M.D., "Is There a Male Climacteric?" *Geriatrics,* X (April, 1955) 40–73.

5. Joseph B. Trainer, *Physiologic Foundations for Marriage Counseling* (St. Louis: C. V. Mosby Co., 1965), p. 95.

6. Wilhelm Stekel, *Impotence in the Male* (New York: Liveright Publishing Co., 1939), I, 1–5.

7. Helen Deutsch, *Psychology of Women* (New York: Grune & Stratton, Inc., 1945), II, 459 and 475.

8. *Ibid.,* p. 459.

9. *Ibid.,* p. 475.

10. Masters and Ballow, *loc. cit.*

11. Hess, Roth, and Kaminsky, *op. cit.,* p. 47.

CHAPTER 5—SEXUAL SUCCESS IN THE MID-YEARS

1. Edmund Bergler, *The Revolt of the Middle-Aged Man* (New York: Hill & Wang, Inc., 1958), p. 2.

2. *Ibid.,* p. 86.

3. *Ibid.,* p. 311.

4. Gordon Cumming, "A Study of Marital Conflicts Involving an Affair by One of the Partners" (Unpublished master's thesis, University of Southern California, Los Angeles, 1960), p. 61.

5. John Cuber and Peggy Harroff, "The More Total View: Relationships Among Men and Women of the Upper Middle Class," *Marriage and Family Living*, XXV (May, 1963), 140–45.

6. *Ibid.*, pp. 142–43.

7. Maxine Davis, *Sexual Responsibility in Marriage* (New York: Dial Press, 1963), p. 221.

8. William H. Masters, M.D., and Virginia E. Johnson, *Human Sexual Response* (Boston: Little, Brown & Co., 1966), p. 240.

9. *Ibid.*, p. 262.

10. Emily H. Mudd, Howard E. Mitchell, and Sara B. Taubin, *Success in Family Living* (New York: Association Press, 1965), p. 122.

11. Joseph B. Trainer, *Physiologic Foundations for Marriage Counseling* (St. Louis: C. V. Mosby Co., 1965), p. 217.

12. Jessie Bernard, "Developmental Tasks of the NCFR—1963–1988," *Journal of Marriage and the Family*, XXVI (February, 1964), 33–34.

CHAPTER 6—MAKING THE MOST OF THE MID-YEARS

1. Robert J. Havighurst, "Middle-Age—The New Prime of Life," in *Aging in Today's Society*, ed. Clark Tibbitts and Wilma Donahue (Englewood Cliffs, N. J.: Prentice-Hall, Inc., 1960), pp. 137 ff. Although the precise statement of the points discussed in this section is made by Havighurst, he credits Robert F. Peck for the basic formulation of these comments about aging.

2. This material was presented in a gerontology seminar at the University of Southern California, spring, 1967, by Dr. James Birren, executive director of the Rossmoor-Cortese Institute for the Study of Retirement and Aging.

3. Havighurst, *op. cit.*, p. 145.

4. John Walker Powell, "Life's Changing Tasks" in *ibid.*, p. 156.

5. (Boston: Houghton Mifflin Co., 1938).

6. (Philadelphia: J. B. Lippincott Co., 1957).

7. (New York: Charles Scribner's Sons, 1964).

8. (New York: W. W. Norton & Co., 1964).

9. (Princeton, N. J.: D. Van Nostrand Co., Inc., 1962).

10. (Boston: Little, Brown & Co., 1966).

11. Arthur Jersild, *The Psychology of Adolescence* (New York: The Macmillan Co., 1957), pp. 201–3.

12. (New York: Alfred A. Knopf, Inc., 1955).

13. J. I. Simmons and Barry Winograd, *It's Happening* (Santa Barbara, Calif., Marc-Laird Publications, 1966), pp. 12–30.

14. Edgar Z. Friedenberg, *The Vanishing Adolescent* (New York: Dell Publishing Co., Inc., 1965), pp. 179–85.
15. Marvin Sussman, "The Isolated Nuclear Family: Fact or Fiction?" *Social Problems*, VI (1959), 333–40.

CHAPTER 7—ANTICIPATION OF THINGS TO COME

1. Wilma Donahue, Harold L. Orback, and Otto Pollack, "Retirement: The Emergent Social Pattern," in *Handbook of Social Gerontology*, ed. Clark Tibbitts (Chicago: University of Chicago Press, 1960), p. 378.
2. *Ibid.*
3. *Ibid.*, p. 390.
4. Memorandum (Washington: Administration on Aging, Department of Health, Education and Welfare, 1966), p. 1.
5. *Ibid.*, p. 64.
6. *Ibid.*, p. 65.
7. Eugene A. Confrey and Marcus S. Goldstein, "The Health Status of Aging People," in Tibbitts, *op. cit.*, p. 187.
8. *Ibid.*, p. 202.
9. Robert J. Havighurst, "Flexibility and Social Roles of the Retired," *American Journal of Sociology*, LIX, 311.
10. J. E. Anderson, "Psychological Aspects of the Use of Free Time," in *Free Time: Challenge to Later Maturity*, ed. Wilma Donahue, Dorothy H. Coons, and Helen K. Maurice (Ann Arbor: University of Michigan Press, 1958), p. 41.

CHAPTER 8—THE CHOICE IS YOURS

1. Bernice Neugarten, "A New Look at Menopause," *Psychology Today*, I, No. 7, 43.
2. *Ibid.*, p. 44.

Index

155